READY
FOR
BATTLE

By the same author:

Born for Battle:
  31 Studies on Spiritual Warfare

Ready
for
Battle
31 Studies in Christian Discipleship

R. Arthur Mathews

OM PUBLISHING
Carlisle, U.K.

British Library Cataloguing in Publication Data

Mathews, R. Arthur
Ready for Battle: 31 Studies in Christian Discipleship
I. Title
248.4

ISBN 1-85078-143-5

OM Publishing is an imprint of Send the Light Ltd.,
PO Box 300, Carlisle, Cumbria, CA3 0QS, U.K.

Published in association with OMF Books, Belmont,
The Vine, Sevenoaks TN13 3TZ, U.K.

Printed in the U.K. by Cox and Wyman Ltd., Reading.

Contents

Preface vii

1. Going After Jesus 1

2. The Call of God 5

3. No Refusal Rights 11

4. Finding Yourself 15

5. Spiritual Navigation 19

6. The Need and the Call 23

7. When We Can't See 27

8. Guarding Our Potential 31

9. Your God Is Too Soft 35

10. Am I Missionary-Minded? 39

11. Put Your Shoes On! 43

12. The Camels Are Coming! 47

13. Excalibur, Two-sided Sword 53

14. Search for Identity 57

15. Finding God's Exact Will 61

16. Our Role 65

17. Faith's Alternate 69

18. Total toward Him 75

19. Candidate for Dying 79

20. Opportunity Price Tag 83

21. Time and the Towel 87

22. Wrestling 91

23. Sent to Reap 95

24. The "Now" Factor 99

25. When We Are "De-elected" 103

26. Divine Designation 107

27. Living That Counts 111

28. Life's Impact 115

29. Beyond Training 119

30. Divine Perspective 123

31. Smiths, Spoilers, and Soldiers 127

Preface

Two destinies are open to us in life—tragedy or triumph, to finish up a misfit or to find fulfillment. We come to either of these destinies, not by blind chance or good luck, nor by some freak of fate, but by our own choices. At life's crossroads we make decisions that take us onto the high road of triumph and fulfillment or onto the low road of tragedy.

For each of us God has a "good and acceptable and perfect will"—the ultimate of love's planning. And for this will he equips us, endowing us with the capabilities for doing just that and not something else. He has designed both the dispositions we have and the ring of circumstances in which we find ourselves that we might travel the high road of his will, bringing him maximum glory. No other will, no product of human intuition or intelligence can achieve that goal by itself. Every talent or faculty shunted off the track God designed for it will inevitably end up botched by misuse or lost by disuse and stand as a monument to the tragedy of choosing the low road. These pages are dedicated to helping God's children find and choose the high road.

R. Arthur Mathews

1

Going After Jesus

The Resorter and the Follower

Jesus Christ was an exciting person. When he hit a town, crowds exploded into the streets. The young and old, the ill and the well, the critical and the curious all swarmed around him.

But there was another difference that divided the crowd that surrounded this central figure. Mark 2:13-14 says, "The multitude resorted unto [Jesus]. . . . Levi . . . followed him" (KJV). The reporter sorts out the two categories and puts them in close proximity to each other as if to invite a study of the contrasts: the multitude and Matthew (who is called Levi in this passage); the crowd who resorted to Jesus and, standing over against them, the lonely follower.

Both resorters and followers are found today where Jesus Christ is at work. And the in-depth stir that focused on the historic Lord is, in fact, being repeated on the contemporary scene, especially among the young. Even the secular press is impressed. The contrast between the resorters and the followers in the crowd is obvious. But it may help us to look at them more closely.

The resorters go along with Jesus Christ on their own terms. At no point are they going to give up their rights. Their own convenience governs the degree of their involvement. Self is the center of their world and controls their motivation and their loyalties. If there is an advantage in going after Jesus, the resorters will be there to collect their tuna sandwich—or loaves and fishes, if you will. But that does not mean they will take a stand against the crowd that is demonstrating against Jesus and working out its hate in campaigning to have him crucified. Oh, no!

The resorters are amazed at what Jesus does. They are attracted to the light as a moth is drawn to the candle. If he is lonely, he is impressed by the genuine love Jesus shows for society's rejects. If she is young, she is excited by the challenge Jesus poses to traditionalists fighting to maintain the status quo. If he is one of the sick, he is attracted by the fact that Jesus performs miraculous cures without charge.

But though the resorters come in a mixed bag, they do have this in common with fellow resorters: they are neither committed to the person of Jesus Christ, nor unreservedly involved with him in his cause.

The follower is a person who knows what it is to have a confrontation of wills with Jesus Christ and to yield to him as Lord. Matthew was such a man.

Sensing a crowd in the offing on the day our text describes, Matthew looked up from his desk at the customs gate. His eyes were held. Jesus was looking at him, searching his soul, reading him through and through. The place was the noisy, dusty street of Capernaum, not the sanctum of the synagogue. No soft music was playing to precondition him psychologically for a public confession of discipleship.

In the hot glare of the sun Matthew was facing an audience more hostile than friendly, more ready to criticize than to sympathize. Two words cut through the babble of the crowd: "Follow me."

The moment was electric. The noisy jabber of the resorters simmered down until suddenly there was complete, awkward silence. Jesus was claiming tax collector Matthew—one of the most hated men in town. All eyes focused on the traitor. Would self-consideration in the man overrule the higher claim?

The volume of chatter picked up again. The confrontation was over. Matthew had joined the ranks of the followers. He had sold out to Jesus Christ and burned his bridges. It cost him just as much as it will cost you—everything.

2

The Call of God

The Predictable and the Unpredictable

The whole subject of personal guidance is one that deeply concerns serious-minded Christians today. One professor told me that this was at the top of the list of problem areas for the young people that come to him for counsel. It is unfortunate that the most important thing in a young person's life should be so smothered with uncertainty. Tragically much of this uncertainty and confusion has been created by brash statements of well-meaning missionaries. Instead of throwing light on the search of young people for realities in this mystical area, dogmatists continue to sound off their mutually contradictory opinions. These have smothered the subject under a dense smoke screen, effectively smudging out definitive lines, particularly the part that concerns "the call of God."

Sorry, young people, we owe you our apologies!

While I may not be able to clarify what has been confused, I do want to help you discover for yourselves the validity of a category that is being lost. Our lost glory is in the decline of those who can boast as the apostle Paul boasted—"God made me a minister." The backbone of any missionary group is surely the core of workers who glory in their office and testify with certainty that as missionaries they belong to the God-made category.

Without doubt Paul was a God-made missionary. From birth he was separated to fulfill the eternal purpose of God. He was theologically persuaded as to the rightness of his task. And he was directed to a specific people with a significant message.

But how, in practical terms, did Paul know that he was called of God and called to the Gentiles? How was he convinced that he was God's chosen man for this particular work, and not Peter or Philip? How did he get the assurance he needed to maintain his direction against strong currents of popular opinion?

As a new convert, Paul—or as he was known then, Saul—was concerned with the life guidance question. "What shall I do, Lord?" was his question. " 'Get up,' the Lord said, 'and go into Damascus. There you will be told all that you have been assigned to do' " (Acts 22:10). So Paul was looking for God's specific answer.

But for him, as for each person looking for God's way, there was both a predictable and an unpredictable direction. The predictable direction for Paul pointed to a life of work among the Jews. It would seem stupid to ignore the education he had received in Jersualem at the feet of the great Gamaliel by spending his life evangelizing the Gentile world. Furthermore, Paul's sympathies were with his own people. His heart surged and stormed within him over their lostness. He longed after them with great heaviness. His burden for them was so great, in fact, that he said he could wish himself "cursed and cut off from Christ" for their sakes. Surely these strong feelings had some significance in terms of his life's predictable direction. If we were to make our judgment, we would not hesitate to decide that Paul was so eminently qualified for work with the Jews that it would be wrong to send him out to organize a program of world evangelism among non-Jews.

But because a course in life seems right and reasonable, it does not follow that it is God's will. God does not tie himself to the obvious. There is an unpredictable element in guidance that defies logic, that will not conform to our neat thought patterns. God will be God.

Yet when God has given his person direction, even though confronted with the unpredictable, that person will be able to move out to face friend or foe with an unshakable certainty that "God made me a servant." It might not be in the predictable direction they once thought, but "according to [God's] eternal purpose which he purposed in Christ Jesus our Lord." They will be able to stand before church council or candidate committee and assert: "It was not my initiative, but God's sovereign selection. It was not my preference, but God's choosing. It is not anything in me; it is God's grace gift. God willed, and I obeyed. God called, and I followed. God revealed, and I saw. God made me his servant, and I glory in my calling."

But how, in the beginning, did God bring Paul to abandon the idea of working among his own people? Before any of God's servants are ready to scrap the predictable direction, there has to be some drastic, some overmastering intrusion. What was it for Paul? First and foremost, there had to be a theological reorientation. Paul had to be made to see in the Scriptures that God was the God not only of the Jew, but also of the non-Jew. He had to see that his people were betraying the Gentile world, denying them a part in the grace that was equally for all. Paul had to be convinced of the theological validity of his service role to the Gentiles. God did convince him—in his Word. In Isaiah, Hosea, Psalms, and 2 Samuel Paul clearly saw the Lord's wider purposes.

If we are to find the apostle's path to assurance, it might help to sketch out some of the steps:

1. He started right by asking, "What shall I do, Lord?"

2. He saw his job description and service category in the Scriptures, and God offered it to him as a gift.

3. He was praying and heard God say, "Go; I will send you far away to the Gentiles" (Acts 22:21).

4. His special call was confirmed by others. God told godly Ananias of Damascus that Paul was his chosen instrument to bear his name among the Gentiles (Acts 9:15). And Paul wrote to the Galatians, "James, Peter and John . . . recognized the grace given to me. They agreed that we should go to the Gentiles, and they to the Jews" (Gal. 2:9).

5. His suitability for his particular service was confirmed by the Holy Spirit. Paul testifies, "For God, who was at work in the ministry of Peter as an apostle to the Jews, was also at work in my ministry" (Gal. 2:8).

Can you say, "God made me his minister?" Is he, by any chance, trying to show you his unpredictable direction? Confirmation will come in the serious study of the Word coupled with prayer. It may require a period of heart searching and travail. But when God is ready, he will produce in you an assurance that he has a way and a place for you and will reveal the steps ahead.

3

No Refusal Rights

Challenging the Challenge

How imperative is the imperative? To what degree can we dilute an imperative and leave it still a command? Or is the structure of the imperative impervious to dilution and incapable of being weakened? It is my contention that while we may play around with grammar rules and make exceptions to suit ourselves, we cannot change the intention of the Savior when he uttered his "Go!"

The recruitment technique commonly practiced today follows the challenge-volunteer method. By using this missionary-challenge approach, we have unintentionally and unconsciously substituted a lower standard than God intends.

Let us scrutinize this challenge-volunteer technique. We are all acquainted with the voice of the challenger, sometimes pleading, sometimes denouncing. Always, it seems, the attention moves from the speaker to the addressed and then focuses on those from the group that volunteer. The volunteer takes the stage while the Lord Jesus is unconsciously moved to one side. The young person is given a choice: If she accepts the challenge, the prize includes distinction, kudos, the praise of other people. On the other hand, if she refrains from making an offer, she will not be singled out for particular blame; she is safely hidden in the crowd (except perhaps in her own mind).

The challenge method sparks the wrong motivation. It leaves the car in neutral while the volunteer makes up his or her mind. Instead of demanding an immediate response, it tolerates delay. It avoids the imperatives that the Scriptures insist on. Thus while Jesus Christ commands, "Go," the challenge permits an alternate and preferred reading—"Won't you go?"—thus switching the unqualified imperative into a meek and negotiable interrogative. By allowing a rationalizing of the implications of Christ's command, it quiets the voice of conscience.

What about the command-obey approach to missionary recruiting? The demands of this method are far more exacting. We are confronted with "the Lord of the harvest." He is accorded the authority to command and the central place in the program of recruitment. Christians, the little heroes of the challenge-volunteer scheme—with their hesitation, uncertainty, and fitful bursts of enthusiasm—are forced into the subordinate place, which is their rightful place. They are yielded no refusal rights to any command the Lord issues, for they are not expected to frame answers other than yes. No draft-board categories provide them with a way out.

In this command-obey program the sovereign Lord is stating an imperative. Neither the passage of time nor the change of circumstances can alter the intention of the one who is "the same yesterday, and today, and forever." From the platform of supreme authority, his intention was to place the requirement for obedience on all to whom the word applies. His intention was to eliminate the necessity for knotty choices.

We, on the other hand, have substituted the I'll-think-it-over-and-pray-about-it reflex for unhesitating obedience. The motivation for service is Calvary-quickened love that expresses itself in absolute loyalty. For the one redeemed by the blood of Christ there is no justifiable alternative to obedience. The issue for the believer is as sharp in contrast as black and white—it is to obey or to disobey, to respond or to rebel.

The greatest need today is for evangelical Christians to recover the obedience reflexes that have been so largely lost. O that we might experience a renewal of heart devotion to Jesus Christ that acknowledges him as Lord! O that love for him might empty us of our shallow desires for self-expression and fill us with a longing to please him, to go in the way of his commandments!

4

Finding Yourself

Don't Melt Your Candle for Tallow

The jingle we sang as kids with its accompanying sign language—an agitated vertical index finger—taught us what we were supposed to do with "this little light of mine." We were to let it shine! A more sophisticated source, George Eliot, tells us what not to do, and I quote: "Don't let your candle be melted down for tallow. Learn how to find yourself." Perhaps it is not easy for you to connect candles and tallow with finding yourself. But believing a connection exists, I want us to try to find it. If we can, we will have an answer to a question confronting many people today.

Concerned to find ourselves, we ask: What am I here for? Where am I going? What purpose is there in life? To these questions George Eliot gives a good answer—a good answer because it is just what Jesus Christ said.

A candle is manufactured for the express purpose of giving light. When the electricity is cut off, a candle finds itself. Shining in the context of a crisis of darkness, it realizes its true vocation; it achieves fulfillment; it finds purpose, candle purpose.

To melt down candles for tallow is to court frustration in the hour of crisis. A man stumbling around in the dark and hopelessly lost is not going to get excited over a lump of tallow. Anyone who would melt a candle for its fat content must be either blind or a fool. A blind person cannot use light. A fool thinks the darkness is a myth. It is the fool or the blind one, then, that wastes the candle in order to produce a useless lump of fat.

But today, more than ever, God's candles are being melted down for tallow. Christian young people are being encouraged to devote time and energy to purposes unrelated to the context of the crisis of their times. In the place of candle purpose, which is labeled unrealistic or impractical, they are introduced to the idea of candle presence, as though that holds all the answers for people in the dark.

The Savior's statement "You are the light of the world" indicates the true context and significance of the world's crisis. All people are in darkness. They are hopelessly lost without the true light. Candle presence is not enough. Melted-down tallow is irrelevant to the problem.

The world can cry, "We're here to educate, not to convert," but when the Christian takes up the chant, he is melting his candle for tallow. In shining, God's people find themselves, though they burn up in doing it. By the same token, they lose themselves when they substitute any other activity for bearing light and giving significant witness.

- Self-chosen functions, if they are ignored or are given preeminence over God's appointed function, are destructive of spiritual fiber.

- Self-chosen vocations create misfits in God's eternal scheme of things.

- Self-chosen appointments misread the context of spiritual darkness in which men apart from Christ live and die.

Lost people need light before literacy, new hope before a new home. Don't melt your candle down for tallow. Recapture God's candle purpose for your "little light," and find yourself.

5

Spiritual Navigation

The Hazard of the Uncorrected Compass

How is it that Christians often seem to mistake God's leading? One person is positive that he should serve God as a witness in a secular position overseas, and nothing will move him from this conviction. Another is equally sure that God wants her to serve as a full-time missionary somewhere. Yet there is a good chance that neither of these will ever get to the envisioned destination. Why? How can a man or woman be sure at any given point that his or her conviction is from God and is therefore reliable?

In navigating a ship from one harbor to another the shipmaster must rely on a compass. But the shipmaster has to know first that the compass has been protected from the internal magnetic field of the ship itself; otherwise it will give a distorted reading. To give a true reading, a compass must be free from all other pulls, so that it is free to respond to the earth's magnetic field. It is not enough for the mariner to say, "I have a compass." The shipmaster must know that, in the fitting of the compass in the ship, all the attractions inherent in the ship itself have been nullified and prevented from exerting any deflecting influences.

So it is for the Christian. It is not enough just to be able to say, "I have the Word of God." That person must know that the reading of that Word has not been distorted by his or her own internal magnetic field. When a young person writes to a mission's candidate coordinator and says, "I know it is the will of God for me to apply to your organization," does the candidate secretary dare accept this as the statement that ends all controversy? Not usually. The candidate coordinator knows that there is a strong chance that the words, though spoken in all honesty, may have been uncorrected guidance—i.e., guidance read as true, but with a compass that has been exposed to self's particular interest, a compass distorted by the person's own magnetic field.

It is possible to read the Word of God with an inner attraction that inclines the meaning slightly in the direction of a person's own desires. I know from experience. Under the duress and stress of being under house arrest in Communist China, what I wanted more than anything else was to escape out of all the pressures. My own magnetic field interpreted everything in terms of escape from China. If I saw the swallows heading south, I thought of their good fortune in being able to fly freely to another land. To see a little stick of wood floating down the creek was to start a train of thought that would follow the stick down through all the miles, out into the freedom of the ocean.

Under these conditions even my reading of Scripture was affected. Any verse or passage that had any bearing at all on the idea of escape or that had some word about leaving the country leaped out from the page, and I seized upon it as spoil. I could have built—and at times did—a strong case for believing that it was the will of God for me to get out of China immediately. But this was a distorted reading. The Lord, I believe, was teaching me principles for discerning his will.

Perhaps you react to the above asking, Who then can be sure? How can I know that my reading of the Word of God has not been influenced by my own wishes? Take heart! The Scripture says, "The meek will he guide in judgment: and the meek will he teach his way" (Ps. 25:9, KJV).

Meekness is the opposite of self-assertion. The meek person is the one in whom the pull of self has been so dealt with that the will is free and the mind is open to respond without interference to the magnetic field of the Word of God.

Yes, you say, but that ideal seems too theoretical, too far out of reach. In practical terms, how does a person handle the things in his life that make compass readings on the will of God unreliable? "Carefully divest yourself of your own wishes on the matter," someone wisely counseled, as a start. Self-assertiveness, emotional fixations, likes and dislikes—all need to be resolutely put out of range of influencing the reading of the Word.

In my own case, I allowed my fears to control my desires. So strong was the pull from this emotional center that it constituted a formidable distortion, even to the point of making God's Word appear to point in the exact opposite direction, south instead of north.

To correct this wrong reading in my case required a major spiritual crisis. My will had to be reset to be resolutely focused on learning what was fully pleasing to the Lord. Once my compass was freed to respond to the Lord's mind, I could easily see how my fears and desires had been blinding me to the obvious. Surely, since God had put me in

Communist China, he must intend me to stay there for his purpose until his time was fulfilled. I have never forgotten that lesson in spiritual navigation.

You have your compass. Just make sure that it is free to swing to God's true north, undistorted by self's attractions.

6

The Need and the Call

Discovering God's Imperatives

When need pounds at my door, is the need itself the signal that God intends me to answer the door, roll up my sleeves, and give myself to meeting that need? In other words, does need that I can meet obligate me to respond to it?

I say that the presence of need ought to push me to seek the presence of God—to hear from him concerning what his priorities are. Responding to need as if it by itself constitutes the call of God consigns me to a life of frustration and unnecessary stress.

No, if the voice of God is drowned in the noise pollution of the good thing that I am doing, then the greater need is to pull away from earth's feverish impulses and with God in the quiet of the soul's solitude to capture for myself a conviction of what his imperatives are for me. Let me illustrate what I am saying from a situation early in the ministry of the Lord Jesus.

It had been a busy Sabbath, in the Capernaum synagogue first, and then in the home of Peter's mother-in-law. As the Syrian sun set in the dusky west, signaling the end of the Sabbath, "all the city was gathered together at the door" (Mark 1:33, KJV). The need was clamant. The lame, the diseased, the blind—in fact, the sum total of Capernaum's clinical needs were pressing with presumptive insistence about the doorway of the house where Jesus was staying. What they wanted was healing. What they wanted he had.

In view of the Savior's subsequent actions, we dare not assume that the need and the power to meet that need constitutes a call. It takes more than a thronged doorway to indicate what life's direction is to be. It takes more than a special ability to meet the need at the doorway to decree where those abilities are to be applied. Guidance has another ingredient.

As a new day dawned in Capernaum, the disciples were aroused by the calls of people looking for the wonder-healer. But where had he gone? His sleeping mat was empty and cold. One of the twelve sleepily remembered that "very early in the morning" there had been a stirring in the house. He must have gone out to pray. Eventually they tracked him down in a quiet spot in the desert.

"Everyone is looking for you!" they said, their excitement tinged with reproach. They were excited because their master had made a hit. He had the star piece in the act, and the crowd wanted a repeat performance. Instant success? The disciples liked it and wanted more.

But there was something in the master's attitude that was incomprehensible to their dull minds. Jesus did not seem to be responding with enthusiasm to the news that everyone was looking for him. In fact, they had their hands full trying to "keep him from leaving them" (Luke 4:42).

Instead of going back with them to capitalize on the opportunity, he was pressing to get away from the hands that were trying to pull him back to Capernaum. His final word was convincing, completely disarming them. He said, "I must preach . . . to other towns also, because that is why I was sent."

For our Lord, the very need was the call to get alone with God to find his Father's imperatives for him. Heaven's "must" carried the priority and the authority. It overruled all other considerations.

For the man or woman seeking to serve God, there are always two things to be considered. First, *the door of opportunity*. Here one's gifts can be used to the greatest advantage. No one will criticize the person who is pouring out his or her life and talents at Capernaum's doorway. Opportunity, with the gifts to handle it, secures against being a misfit in God's service. Serving at this door promises success, fulfillment, and popularity. Reason says, This is good; therefore it is right.

Second, *the desert perspective*. Jesus was not satisfied with the conclusions of reason. While *vox populi, vox Dei*—the voice of the people is the voice of God—may be good Latin, it is poor theology. Popular demand does not spell divine purpose. Jesus, more than any, knew what was in humanity and was not ready to yield himself to popular demand, even though it did represent real need. He wanted the divine perspective. As a man "under authority," he did not consider it within his rights to form his own opinion and then to do his own thing on the basis of that opinion.

So it was that when Peter and the disciples found him, his mind was made up. He was in the grip of a conviction that would not be gainsaid. On the strength of what he had learned on his knees in the desert place, he forsook the "right" thing in order to do the imperative thing.

Are you swayed by the rightness of some need? If so, before you make your final decision, remember the need is to hear from God's perspective what his priority is vis-à-vis the opportunity that is knocking at your door. You have the Lord's example: "And in the early morning, while it was still dark, He arose and went out and departed to a lonely place, and was praying there" (Mark 1:35, NASB). So when the whole city is at the door, make sure you find your way to the desert.

7

When We Can't See

Obeying without Contingency Plans

Sometimes we would give anything to know what turn events are going to take. To quiet our fears, we long for a keyhole to peep through for a glimpse of what's ahead.

A craving for certainty is particularly aggravated when an important decision confronts us. From the comparative security of a constricted family or church orbit, young people look out on a world where "nation wildly looks at nation" and where "the travail of the ages wrings earth's systems to and fro." With perhaps more than a trace of a shudder, they realize that if life is to count for God out there, they must make the right decisions. But what are the right decisions?

In the search for answers it is all too possible for practical considerations to obscure spiritual realities. A first-century command to "go and make disciples of all nations" may seem outdated and unreal in the twentieth-century world, especially when that world appears to have more drawn curtains than open doors. Nations, fiercely jealous of their sovereign rights, for instance, often exercise their right to limit the presence of Christian workers within their borders. Many potential missionaries, seeing in such limitations the end of the opportunity, set about framing a safe, stay-at-home contingency plan. Yet it is in the arena of the nations that the goal of Jesus Christ is to be reached.

Instead of giving answers and assurances to help clear up our delusions, the Bible is strangely silent. But not without good reason. All that God has included in or caused to be omitted from the Bible is purposely designed to teach a race of calculating humans, strongly influenced by reason and emotions, that goal-fulfillment in God's will is achieved only by the spiritual verities of faith and obedience. In decision making, we must give spiritual factors priority over natural factors.

When God tested Abraham by asking him to sacrifice Isaac, he gave no explanation to satisfy the demand for reasons that must have tortured Abraham's mind. Nor was any concession made to ease the emotional conflict that must have been tearing him apart. The commands of God have their foundation in realities that have the spiritual and eternal qualities of God himself. They are therefore fulfilled only by spiritual responses. Primarily they are a matter for faith and obedience, not human reason or resources. That is, no doubt, why Scripture passes over the feelings of Abraham and mentions only his obedience.

When God told Israel to go up and possess the land, he did not sit down first to balance the will and skill in Israel, or lack of it, against the strength of the enemy defenses and the size and armor of their giant warriors. Again, when Jesus Christ commanded his disciples to feed the hungry crowd, his order was not based on an estimate of the physical resources available. He was confronting them with a moment of decision that would direct them away from the natural man's responses to his rock-bottom spiritual requirement of obedience and faith. Instead of responding with obedience, however, they tried to draw him down to their level of practical wisdom.

In each case, first Israel and then the disciples, the implications of obedience boggled their shivering wisdom. Israel protested, "The cities are walled up to heaven, and we seemed like grasshoppers in our own eyes." The disciples argued, "All we have are five loaves and two fish." Both these groups treated the goal of God's will as an impossible gamble and so halted, abashed. They failed in goal-fulfillment because they had unspiritual attitudes toward the process involved in attaining the goal. They failed because they were bankrupt in the ability to come up with spiritual responses.

While the command of God relates primarily to God's goal, it does not ignore the process by which the goal is attained. The principle that guarantees that the process will achieve the goal is stated in the words, "He himself knew what he would do" (John 6:6, KJV). It is decision based on and responsive to the eternal fact and sufficiency of God to complete the work he seeks to initiate. To halt and quibble over the process of attainment when God has given a specific command is not sanity or humility; it is rank rebellion.

Hudson Taylor perceived this as he faced the completely unevangelized interior provinces of China in 1864. The church was suffering a bad case of "closed-door-itis" and argued, "We must wait until God's providence opens the door; at present we can do nothing." Hudson Taylor declared, "When the Lord Jesus gives a definite command, is it our place to ask whether it can be fulfilled or not?" He saw that God's commands are issued from a basis of complete knowledge and perfect power, not from a calculated gamble on the chances of success. Because God's commands are never speculative or experimental, he is not required to formulate contingency plans to cover failure.

God never commands the impossible. He never asks for a decision that will involve a gamble. And because of this, what we need to guide us in life is not a peep through some keyhole or a list of explanations to satisfy our minds—we need instead the will to obey against our better judgment and against our strongest emotional inhibitions.

Those who halt short of fulfilling God's will because they are unable to come up with spiritual responses need to learn to pray, "Lord, loosen in me the fear of visible things." To those who will obey regardless of the cost to themselves, the precious partnership of human obedience and divine omnipotence carries this assurance: "With God all things are possible."

For my moment of decision let me say with Madame Guyon:

Thy wonderful, grand will, my God,
With triumph now I make it mine;
And faith shall cry a joyous "yes!"
To every dear command of Thine.

8

Guarding Our Potential

The Holy Spirit, the Great Investor

"If it is so hard for me to find the will of God for my life when I know myself as I do, how can someone else, either individual or group, know with any degree of certainty where God wants me and what he wants me to do?" Obviously the one who wrote this has run afoul of some Christian organization's placement policy and has taken a new look at his guidance.

For most of us the business of discovering where we fit in life is a major concern. From childhood we are fed all sorts of ideas on the life that is opening ahead of us. Our inbuilt computer systems, grooved with inherent likes and dislikes and personality traits, sort these ideas, rejecting some and holding on to others. It is not until we become Christians that we have new spiritual machinery to control the impulses of acceptance or rejection.

But are we shut up to experimentation or computer-type reckoning to find where we fit? Is there no point where we and others involved can be mutually assured that a certain course is God's directive will?

Does God rule, or is he just a convenient overruler to prevent threatened catastrophe when we make the wrong move? Somehow trial-and-error guidance delegates God to a place on our trail while we putter around with our experiments.

Yet if God rules, where do we fit the mistakes that are made, assuming that things do go wrong sometimes? How do we reconcile this with a sovereign God who doesn't make mistakes? Who made the mistake in the case of the first-term missionary casualty, for instance? Was it the mission board's fault for putting him in the wrong place? Perhaps it was. Even spiritual leaders don't claim infallibility. Or was it the fault of the individual in committing himself to a mission board? Perhaps it was. Was he wrongly motivated? Maybe. Or should we blame God for not keeping him from the final breakdown? Hardly, for who would dare lay mistakes at God's door?

While we are at this business of pulling things apart and scattering the pieces, let's look closer at both sides in a missionary casualty case.

Missionary candidates come with gifts, education, qualifications. Their specialized training has fitted them for something specific in life. They feel a sense of responsibility to be a careful steward of their potential. At some point in their life they have committed themselves to serve their generation in the will of God. Their best service, surely, will be rendered along the line of their natural bent and training. Thus they have taken time to search out a missionary opportunity that accords with these factors.

In deciding on a mission agency, young people have investigated carefully. At this stage their automatic rejection unit is ready to dispose of any board that has a record of hijacking. Any indication of mission-empire mentality in a group is enough to trigger them into violent combustion. They are not about to offer themselves as guinea pigs. They want a sympathetic, understanding ear. They want to sense a spirit of cooperation, not control. They want to reason, not to be tied with authoritarian regulations. These young people come defensive, discerning, ready to go if . . . .

The mission organization, on the other hand, is complex, involving a number of lives for which the leaders feel a responsibility before God and a host of interweaving imponderables. Generally these leaders are not unaware of the need for foresight to insure that talents are not wasted and lives not just played with.

But is it always the will of God that the specific training be matched to a specific service opportunity? What was behind the church's best-trained worker for Jewish evangelism being sent off on a church-planting jig among the Gentiles? Was this a hijacking stunt? The Bible doesn't explain much. It simply states, "The Holy Spirit said, 'Set apart for me . . . Saul for the work to which I have called [him]' " (Acts 13:2). Is the Holy Spirit cooperating with the intuitions of Paul? Or does he have a commanding role? Manifestly the church at Antioch had no alternative but to obey. The individual had no opportunity for job selection by talent matching.

Unavoidably, if we are to move ahead to a position of assurance, we must include the Holy Spirit in our thinking. Until now there has been an element of uncertainty in what we have been saying because we have been talking on the level of human mistakes. Confusion and uncertainty, in fact, are the natural outcome of ignoring the Holy Spirit and misplacing his role in our lives. His place is as leader, not follower. His place is not to cooperate with man-centered guidance or with human institutions, for this arrangement forces him into a subordinate role. The Holy Spirit guides, but only on his own terms; he guides where he governs.

To guard our potential in order to invest our lives wisely is not our responsibility, but God's. He does the investing. Lives offered unreservedly to him he invests according to his own will—i.e., Peter to the Jews and Paul among the Gentiles. Those who insist on their own right to invest their gifts for God are contradictions in consecration.

You may still have your questions. It could be that the best answers are positive assertions, for instance, "I believe in the Holy Spirit"—in his sovereignty, in his wisdom, in his office. Computer-matching is for those who don't have the faith to make such assertions. Experiments are for those who have never surmounted life's mistake level. The way to the upper level is by unreserved commitment of life and talent to Jesus Christ and by faith that God has accepted me for investment in his chosen place and among his chosen opportunities. The person with this stance of commitment and faith is bound to find that point of mutual assurance with church and teammates in which all sides hear the Holy Spirit's voice saying, "Set apart for me . . . I have called."

9

Your God Is Too Soft

Leanness via Self-Insistence

Israel wanted a king. Having to obey God inhibited them in doing their own thing. They preferred a visible king to be their leader and to help them fight their enemies.

And, let it be noted, God let them have their way. He didn't argue the point or make an awkward situation out of the fact that they were rejecting him. He was even kind enough to warn them of the trouble they were pulling down on their own heads by choosing a king in his place.

On another occasion the Israelites wanted a change of diet. Tired of their one-course diet of manna, they longed for something to get their teeth into. They wanted meat and stirred up a storm until God gave them quail. Yes, God responded to their complaints and made special provision for them.

Somehow these incidents seem to refute the hell-fire-and-brimstone picture of God that we have been fed. Reading these Old Testament stories encourages us, at least superficially, in the idea that God is soft. In fact, it almost seems as if we can mold God into whatever shape we want. With impunity these men stripped God of his throne. They found an easy way out, a way that relieved them of going through with his will. They boohooed like spoiled kids at the kind of food he gave them, and like spoiled kids seemed to get away with it.

We ask, What sort of God is this that gives in so easily? The critics scoff, the careless couldn't care less, and infantile Christians flaunt their independence. But, as I have inferred, it is a superficial reading that limits our understanding of the total truth. There is more to it than is seen in a hasty scanning of the story.

While God might appear to be soft and easily swayed, there is no surer way to self-injury and ruin than trying to alter God's will to suit our own desires. Such action on our part brings an inexorable principle into operation: Tampering with God's will weakens spiritual life. The psalmist gives his inspired statement of this principle in Psalm 106:15—"he gave them their request; but sent leanness into their soul" (KJV).

You thought Jesus Christ was being unrealistic when he said, "If anyone comes to me and does not hate his father and mother, his wife and children, his brothers and sisters—yes, even his own life—he cannot be my disciple" (Luke 14:26).

You felt that your initial response to the stimulus of God that stirred within you a sense of responsibility to serve him in a certain place or way was an immature impulse. Since then you have rationalized, argued your rights, and found for yourself a job more suited to your training and qualifications. Yet no matter how expansive you might be about the change, you cannot shake off the feeling that your soul has shriveled in the deal.

You argued that consistent church attendance exhausted your responsibility for involvement in spiritual service. You were glad your God was soft enough to let you set your own standards, choose your own pace, and plan your own life. Your God is not dead, but you have stolen his crown, robbed him of his lordship, and all that you have left is a "Convenience," with a capital *C*. The inner, instinctive spirit of the church has been squandered, and the price is being exacted in full. Leanness is in proportion to self-insistence. Let's not kid ourselves: "God cannot be mocked. A man reaps what he sows" (Gal. 6:7).

10

Am I Missionary-Minded?

Jesus Christ as Our Measure

If anyone was missionary-minded, it was Jesus Christ. His activities as teacher, preacher, and healer were manifestations of his missionary vocation. The apostle Paul sees him as the supreme example of the missionary mind and urges his friends at Philippi, "Let this mind be in you, which was also in Christ Jesus" (Phil. 2:5, KJV). And through Paul the Holy Spirit gives us insights into what it is that constitutes missionary-mindedness. We are meant to be aware of the standard God has set and then take it to ourselves.

In Philippians 2 a simple progression emerges:

- What Jesus Christ was—his identity.

- What Jesus Christ thought—his intuition.

- What Jesus Christ did—his initiative.

- What Jesus Christ became—his identification.

The starting point for the missionary mind in our Lord related to his identity. He existed in the form of God. Heaven's culture, with all its purity and privilege, was his lifestyle. He lived in the realms of light in which there was no darkness at all, and he enjoyed the perfect love of a home and a society in which there was no wrangling or bitterness. This was his starting point. It was here the mind came into play, and Paul tells us what his thoughts were: "[He] did not consider equality with God something to be grasped" (Phil. 2:6). God's mission for him had a compelling priority over all considerations of personal status and privilege.

To follow the Savior's example, we must begin where we are. The starting point for the birth and growth of missionary-minded attitudes in us is what we are in our own home circumstances, including the total lifestyle and all the prerogatives and advantages that are part and parcel of those circumstances. These are the things we must reckon with when God's missionary purpose becomes known to us. Instead we tend to focus on what we think the consequences to us will be if we commit ourselves to God's purpose.

Jesus Christ faced the will of God independent of any consequences to himself. Without hesitating to figure out what might happen at the other end, he made himself ready, he "made himself nothing" (Phil 2:7). The principle governing missionary-minded decision making is, "Look not every man on his own things, but every man also on the things of others" (Phil. 2:4, KJV).

The Son's "own things" were the life of pure bliss without complications in the heavenly home. "The things of others" were at the opposite pole and would involve great sacrifice. It would mean moving from the realm of light, love, and purity to that of darkness, hate, and wickedness and exchanging life unlimited for life in the form of a slave. Christ did not cling to his head start, but chose to begin from scratch as an indigenous citizen in earth's culture tangles, identifying with his mission field.

A missionary mind is a mind that is not alienated from the harsh realities of life around us, a mind that chooses to be vulnerable to the haters and the hunters and seeks no foxhole for escape. Foxes have a way of escape; Jesus had none. For his weariness there was no pillow. No manna came down from heaven to allay his hunger pangs. When chased, Jesus looked for no hiding place. So earthlings vented their anger on him and had him crucified, and nothing could persuade him to save himself at the expense of his persecutors.

Culture shock had no power to make him a casualty, and not because he carried cassette tapes of heaven's music or kept a container of heavenly manna in the fridge. His survival resources were not in cultural props, but in a mind that thought only of self-emptying and a will that accepted God's will as his love law.

A missionary mind is a mind that is not absorbed with the legitimate claims of home duties to the exclusion of other claims. Jesus did not argue that the responsibility of controlling the infinite universe of whirling galaxies required his presence. Nor did he plead that the business of gilding the streets and tuning the harps of his hometown was a full-time job and better suited his abilities. The missionary mind has the Cross at its magnetic north and empties itself of all that would deflect its compass.

A missionary mind is a mind that is not ashamed to identify with a foreign culture. It is totally impossible for

41

us to conceive all that was involved in the voluntary self-emptying and self-humbling of the Lord Jesus Christ. We tend to grade other cultures by using our own as the standard, and while we conscientiously work to overcome this tendency, the surrender of first place for our own culture is often grudging and superficial.

Missionaries go overseas but do not always really leave home. Missionary-mindedness is more than a quiet corner of Western civilization, a hot bath, and a light novel in an Eastern country. It is more than self-chosen activity, at home or abroad, regardless of how good or necessary such activity may be. Our activity must be God-directed, as was the Savior's.

The Christ-mind loved through all the selfish barriers of class and color. He chose to have lunch with Zacchaeus, the most despised man in town. He ate with publicans and sinners. He chatted with the Samaritan woman. In short, he never allowed his identity to keep him aloof from people who needed him.

A timid missionary girl may not appreciate rats chewing their way into her sanctuary of mosquito netting, but she stays on in a foreign backwater because the mind of Christ looks not on its own convenience, but on the needs of others. Wrote one missionary director about two of his missionary team: "What impresses me with [this couple] is their complete identification with the people, the simplicity of their living accommodation, and the two-way communication of Ron's teaching." These are examples of Christ-mindedness overseas. But when the Bible says, "Let this mind be in you, which was also in Christ Jesus," we dare not allow any other mind to be in us, whether God's place for us is in a far-off country or in some local neighborhood.

Put Your Shoes On!

Preparedness to Go

W̲hat should I do to prepare myself for Christian service? is the sort of question committed young people throw out to people in the know. Replies they get generally deal with matters of schooling, specialized training, and church-related experience. And this is what young people want to know.

But Paul has something to say on another dimension of preparation in his well-known passage on the Christian's weapons and armor in Ephesians 6. His application reaches wider than the few who are thinking of becoming missionaries. This is because God's laurels are not for the minority who are the activists. In God's way of reckoning, the will counts for the deed and earns his word of praise: "You did well to have this in your heart" (1 Kings 8:18). The deeds may be for the minority, but to will to do is an option for the mass of believers. The feet of the few are directed to other lands to do exploits in Christ's name; for the many there is the great privilege of roaming far afield with the feet of their hearts in strong desire, eager willingness, and prayer. And it could be that if there were more willing to go with the feet of their hearts, there would be more who would go with their physical feet.

So we come to Paul's special word in Ephesians 6:15. "Shod your feet with the preparation of the gospel of peace" (NASB), he urges. This reference to the warrior's sandals in the list of weapons and armor gets scant treatment from many commentators. The word *preparation* in this version is used only once in the New Testament; thus because there are no other references with which to match it, the commentators flounder.

What I did was to hunt up the very first reference to "having your feet shod" and to use that as a guide. I found it in Exodus 12:11. God is giving Moses orders for the observance of the first passover feast and says, "You shall eat it in this manner: with your loins girded, your sandals on your feet" (NASB). Outside the door of the Israelite home the lamb was to be slaughtered. The blood of the sacrificed animal was then to be sprinkled on the lintel and doorposts. Inside, they were to roast the lamb and eat with every sign of readiness to leave home and take to the road on God's mission. The saved people were to be God's going people. And the readiness to go was incumbent on the mass, not the minority.

Christians have enlarged on the blood that saves and the life that sustains, but have neglected the implications of the shod feet. Unfortunately, while all true Christians are saved, only a minority are ready to go for God.

In the New Testament, in speaking of shod feet, Paul is urging all Christians—not just the missionary or minister—to be ready for any surprise. A veteran warrior himself in the spiritual battle, he knew something of the explosive potential for the unexpected in warfare situations.

The lesson of the Allied landings on the Normandy beaches on D-day, World War II, is that the cost of not expecting the unexpected is defeat. The Nazi commanders allowed themselves to be unready at the crucial moment. They were selective in their readiness. What was true for them is true for the Christian warrior: he only is ready who is unselective in his readiness.

It is easy to find good reasons for not going out actively for Jesus Christ. Some have to care for aged parents; others are crippled by some handicap or invalided with some chronic infirmity. Then there are those busy in the educational processes or caught up in the business rat race. Physical conditions may chain my feet, but God is looking at the feet of my heart. All cannot go, but all are commanded to put shoes on the feet of their hearts as a sign of their honest willingness and readiness to go.

In 1949 and 1950, after the takeover by the Communists in China, my feet were chained from going to the Mongols in Northwest China. Yet the feet of my heart were shod with preparedness to go. I had the will to go, and that is what the Lord wants from his people.

Let's face it. The enemy of readiness is the will that qualifies my readiness. I am ready only when my readiness is unselective:

- Unhesitating as to time—ready anytime.

- Unlimited as to place or distance, climate, or conditions—ready for "whatever utmost distance," as Amy Carmichael put it.

- Unqualified as to type of work—ready for "any manner of service" (1 Chron. 28:21, KJV).

- Unreserved as to the demands—ready to serve, "whether by life or by death."

You ask, "What should I do to prepare myself for God's service?" *Put your shoes on!*

When the fireman got
I. out of his flat he
said Get dressed take
your key and put
on your shoes. He
didn't know where he
was going.

Eph 6v15

12

The Camels Are Coming!

God Seeking His Person

Strung together nosepeg to tail, the camel caravan headed northward. In charge of the party, the nameless servant is well aware of the fateful responsibility that rests upon his shoulders. He must make a choice that will affect all nations.

Away to the north, unaware of the movement of circumstances loaded with import for her, Rebekah moves around the narrow circle of daily duties. One day is no different from another. What sort of chance, she might have asked, does a ordinary girl in ordinary circumstances have of finding her real vocation in life? Will God really do something to see that his plan for my life is brought to my doorstep so that I can at least become aware of it? Or am I to be left only and wholly to my wits and will? In other words, is God responsible for my vocation? Or am I? Or if there is a combination of both, where does God begin and end his part of the business, and where do I fit in?

Rebekah is not alone in her quandary, by any means. These are some of the questions that plague the minds of God-fearing people in every age. We can understand God's guiding Abraham or Hudson Taylor, for these men were big enough to deserve special attention. But how about those of us who are small people, buried in the mass of common obscurity and not ever even likely to get into print? Can we be assured that God does know our identity and has a vocation planned for us? Can we be sure that he will take the initiative in engineering circumstances so that his appointment will reach us?

In Genesis 12 only three verses cover God's call of Abram. In Acts 13 only three verses are given to the call of Barnabas and Saul. It seems completely out of proportion that a subject of such importance, involving a man's life vocation, should be recorded with such scant detail. Surely the minds of these men must have been tortured for months as they travailed over the decisions they were having to make.

But if scant reference is made to God's dealings with these men and their life appointments, not so with his leading of Rebekah. Sixty-seven verses are given to her story in Genesis 24. God is determined that the world's small people shall know of his interest to them and his working of circumstances to bring his plans to them. Take courage—the camels are coming. God is moving over the horizon of your life just as he moved over the horizon for Rebekah.

Whatever God had in mind for Rebekah was a closed book to her. Her life was circumscribed, concerned with household chores and local events. No amount of prognostication on her part would disperse the mists of obscurity that hid life's future from her understanding. She had her own thoughts, her likes and dislikes. Though she probably knew what she wanted, she didn't know God's thoughts.

Our knowledge is further advanced than Rebekah's. We know, at least, that God has a predetermined plan of good works for those created new in Christ Jesus. We know God is the God of appointments. He has a "complete and perfect plan cherished (in his heart for every man)—some exact thing which it will be the true significance of life to accomplish" (H. Bushnell). It is this "exact thing" that we want to discover.

But most of Rebekah's story focuses on the doings of the selector-servant. It does so in such a way as to point out the importance and place of qualifications in the choice to be made. Acting under authority, the servant was to seek, select, and separate a bride for Isaac. That there was someone for this position he had no doubt, for God had promised Abraham that in his seed the nations of the earth were to be blessed. The servant's problem was to locate the girl and to make sure that she had the right qualities to be the wife of Abraham's heir.

The servant halts his dusty camel train at a well outside the city of Haran. Here he sets the stage to suit his purposes. He has chosen the place where the town girls come unposed for the carrying out of a common daily chore.

I used to think that in asking that the right girl offer a draw of water for him and his camels, the servant was just asking for a sign of God's confirmation. Now I wonder. I feel rather that he is laying down the conditions he will need to see fulfilled before he is ready to declare his choice. He is stating the qualifications, not spreading a fleece. He is requiring that the appointee display a certain attitude in an unrehearsed situation. The conditions are such that in the fulfilling of them the inner heart attitude will be exposed. He is not concerned about cooking skills, dress-making abilities, clothes, measurements, or other things beauty-contest judges might put on the list of qualifications.

Neither is the Holy Spirit, the divine selector, impressed with the outward appearance. Nor is he particularly inter-ested in observing us in posed situations, such as in church. He will not be taken in by some assumed spiritual attitude or accent. Before he chooses, he will pin us down in some unposed secular setting where we are confronted by some commonplace task, and there he will stand to watch.

The qualifications for selection are not external, but internal. The fulfillment of the Spirit's requirements will demonstrate a right inner motivation. In his sight attitude is more important than aptitude. Habitual reaction in ordinary circumstances weighs more than sudden responses to emotional stimuli. Goodness that has become chronic through the disciplined acceptance of life's ordinary duties counts for far more than the exhibition of the exceptional.

Rebekah's response was the response of an unposed willingness to do a distasteful job. Who has ever seen a camel look anything but supercilious? Or smell anything but awful? And what animal can drink more than a thirsty camel? Yet, though ten of these thirsty, smelly, supercilious creatures waited for a drink, Rebekah did not stop to weigh the pros and cons, but got on with the job of drawing water. The approval of the selector was the obvious conclusion. He had discovered in Rebekah the "camels-too" brand of moti-vation he sought.

But the story isn't ended. The camels have come; the vocation Rebekah was appointed for has been presented to her, and now she must react. The servant will not force her to follow him back to Isaac. Her family is incidental. She must choose. She must declare her own choice apart from any outward compulsion. I think the servant knew what her answer would be—for the girl who said, "I will draw," would be the type who would also say, "I will go."

"There is then a proper end for every man's [or woman's] life . . . an end which he is privileged to become, called to become, ought to become; that which God will assist him to become, and that which he cannot miss save by his own fault" (H. Bushnell).

Watch! Your camels are coming!

13

Excalibur, Two-sided Sword

Taking and Yielding

Let me introduce you to Excalibur, the sword of King Arthur. This was no ordinary blade. Engraved on one side were the words, "Take me!" And on the other side what we would least expect to see: "Cast me away!" What a contradiction. What knight would be brash enough to throw away that on which his life depended?

Today's Excalibur is not the literal bejewelled sword of Tennyson's King Arthur. It represents in our world the training, knowledge, and skill a person must have if he or she is to act with authority in a given situation. It is one's equipment for facing life and fulfilling high purposes. It is a wise person who heeds the advice to take this Excalibur.

But does the "Cast-me-away" bit apply? How in the world are we to accomplish anything if we deliberately throw away the one thing we have been at such pains to acquire? How are these two contradictory concepts to be reconciled? While we naturally see the "Take me" and the

"Cast me away" as contradictory, from the divine viewpoint they are complementary. They belong to each other.

Yet it is here that young people come up against some of their most desperate conflicts. The mind of the graduate balks at the suggestion that these patent contradictions are part of each other and not to be separated. The temptation at this point is to flare up and go ahead ignoring the "Cast-me-away" line. He argues that since so much has been invested in his training, to throw it away is senseless.

The world has one answer—God has another. The world's Excalibur has only one message on it: "Take me!" But God's Excalibur has the second message on it: "Cast me away!" God is waiting for those who have taken Excalibur to throw it back to the hand that gave it. The weapon he gave needs to be yielded back to him in token of the surrender to the higher authority.

We equate training and qualification. So did Moses. He had a job confronting him that would have boggled a computer. When he was forty years of age, "educated in all the wisdom of the Egyptians," the smoldering consciousness that God had prepared him to lead his people out of bondage burst into full assurance. Moses thought "his own people would realize that God was using him to rescue them" (Acts 7:25).

There's not much glamor in this part of the story—a murder, a grave in the sand, and rejection by his own people. Excalibur—Moses' training in Egypt—far from helping him "fulfill the boundless purposes of [his] king," became an instrument of failure in his hand. The training inspired self-confidence, blinded his eyes to God's perspective, goaded him to precipitate action, and called the plays as it interpreted the need of the moment. But the bubble burst. His large-hearted intent fizzled. No one had accepted him; his own people hadn't believed him, and with a red light flashing in his mind, he pushed the panic button and fled to Midian and the wilderness.

Moses was trained, but he was not yet qualified. Forty years later the real story begins, with God calling him to action, and Moses completely emptied of self-confidence. What things were gain to him he has learned to count as loss. Now he qualified as an appointee for God's mission.

Nearer our time, in the years following World War I, a young Chinese, John Sung by name, came to the States to study. In 1926, with a list of degrees after his name, he boarded the ship for home. Crossing the Pacific, he heard God's still small voice saying, "Cast them away!" God was forcing him to turn his Excalibur over and read the words on the reverse side. Dr. Sung had been enthusiastic enough about getting his training. He was terribly reluctant to let it go. In the bow of the ship, facing the challenge of service, he struggled to hold on to his treasure. The bitter struggle ended as in desperation he took his diplomas and awards and, tearing them to shreds, scattered the pieces to the four winds.

That was one way of doing it—a literal way and a typically John Sung way. But, as radical as his action was, it did demonstrate outwardly the reality of the inner transaction between himself and God. In yielding up his sword to God, he changed categories. The trained man became transformed into God's qualified man. It was this act—the inner act of counting everything but loss for Christ—that qualified John Sung to be the flame for God in China and throughout Southeast Asia.

God gives the best training for the work he has planned for us to do. But only as that training is given back to him in surrender will it be usable in his service. Kept in our hand, the brilliant, diamond-studded Excalibur becomes an instrument of failure. So—

> *"Force me to render up my sword,*
> *And I shall conqueror be."*

14

Search for Identity

The "Belonging" Factor

One man cries, "God, who am I?" Another asserts, "God, . . . whose I am." For the one life is a question, a search for identity. One searches; the other is sure. One lives enshrouded in uncertainty; the other glows with a positive assurance. One spends life with longing; the other with belonging.

I see these two people in the Scriptures. There is the person who is full of questions, the identity seeker, who is impatient with the emptiness of life and its lack of fulfillment. To this person, life—in its own context and unrelated to anything outside of itself—is just "a shadow that passes away," grass that withers, a soon-to-perish flower. Even the originator of the affluent society, the king who made silver and gold as common as dust on the streets of Jerusalem, chose to preach his classic sermon on the text, "Vanity of vanities . . . all is vanity" (Eccles. 1:2, KJV).

By human reasoning Solomon, above all men, had the chance to realize fulfillment—gifted with wisdom more than any man before him, wealthy beyond computation, emotionally satiated with wives accumulated on the permissive I'll-take-whom-I-want basis. Yet he was bored sick with the emptiness of it all.

This man seems unable to escape from the egocentric treadmill. Life's true purpose eludes him either because he cannot or will not break away from himself as the center of his life.

But there is another man. This is the man for whom the search has ended. His feet have left the shifting sands to stand on the rock. His motivation no longer springs from his desires or from his own concepts of what is right and proper. He may end up nailed as a criminal to a Roman gibbet, but it will not be before he has made his claim as did his Lord, "I have brought you glory on earth by completing the work you gave me to do" (John 17:4). Or he may be beaten with rods, scourged with whips, stoned and shipwrecked, hated and hounded, but his last breath will proclaim, "I have finished the race" (2 Tim. 4:7).

The difference between these two categories of people is the "belonging" factor. The identity seekers have not discovered where or to whom they belong. They refuse to accept that God's ownership of them is relevant to life's decisions and choices in the complex pattern of today. They argue that it is all right to be a Christian—that's one side of life. But their Christianity doesn't touch the other side—the need for practical guidance to determine whether life is to be spent as a teacher in Bangkok or a social worker in Chicago. The soul may be set for heaven, but the body is unrelated to that fact, and its course is determined by the whims of upbringing, training, and inclination. Their argument shows that either they are not willing to belong to

God or that they are unaware that such a possibility exists. To these people the Bible says, "I urge you, brothers, in view of God's mercy, to offer your bodies as living sacrifices . . . to God" (Rom. 12:1).

On the other hand, the ones who are committed to Christ and can claim, "God, whose I am and whom I serve," have a different center from which to operate. The God to whom they belong has a plan for their life, specific and in detail. God has made them new creations in Christ and has tooled them for a contemporary function. Society's patterns may undergo revolutionary changes, but God's will for any of his children cannot be uncontemporary or irrelevant.

The relativism of the present age may pronounce against the dogmatism of these people and look askance at them. But with the assurances of God's Word behind them, they can afford to be dogmatic. In the final analysis, the ones who commit themselves to God are the people who can face the world, because they have a sense of belonging, a consciousness of meaningful identity, and a realization of relevant fulfillment.

15

Finding God's Exact Will

No God-provided Alternate

No mother these days—at least in times of prosperity and plenty—would dare call her family to a breakfast table adorned with a single box of cereal. Apart from the capricious taste preferences of individuals, she is aware of the variety of sales gimmicks that are competing to capture the juvenile curiosity and tastebuds of her family. To satisfy her flock these days, Mother has to load her table with a whole range of nut-, raisin-, and sugar-enhanced breakfast foods. The cozy family table is soon followed by the college cafeteria, and by graduation most of us have a built-in resistance to choice limitations.

We cannot, however, blame tastebuds alone for developing our insistence on having our own way. In good things and in bad, "We have turned every one to his own way." We are insistent creatures, and the best of us can be surprisingly stubborn when God allows some circumstances to fence us in.

Satan has it pretty well figured out that even a good person suddenly and inexplicably jerked out of comfortable circumstances will blossom out into a grand case of the sulks, tempted to drop God's way and to go his own. Sulking, of course, is childhood's long-tested technique for getting Mother to weaken her demands. We expect sulking to work with God. Somehow it doesn't.

It is, however, possible to persuade God to the point that he will consent to our self-chosen alternative suggestion to his will. But that doesn't mean he has changed his purpose. God may alter his word to us at our insistence; he will not alter his will for us.

Balaam is a case in point. God's initial ban on his going with Balak's messengers was changed at Balaam's insistence. God did free Balaam from his restrictions, but it was not because he was offering him an alternate way.

Balaam moved progressively away from God's declared will. For this to be personal and applicable to us, we must start with this—God's declared will. Perhaps it seems too narrow a path, but his declared will is where we must start. God does have an exact will for his children. The Bible speaks of God's will as "good, pleasing, and perfect" (Rom. 12:2).

Nowhere is God's will described as being discernable to the natural mind, however. God commits his truth to the heart committed to him, a heart where he reigns.

God is real, personal, alive, and creatively moving in circumstances for the person who "wills to do his will." The Lord deliberately initiates activity in the affairs of this person so that the outer circumstantial evidence, the inner voice of the Spirit, and the plain teaching of the Word all harmonize in assuring the him or her what God's specific will really is. "God said to Balaam, 'Do not go with them' " (Num. 22:12). God's will is clear and unequivocal.

Now let us look at the man as he faces a clearly pronounced directive from God.

First Balaam's mind travels to the "fee for divination" (22:7). Suddenly desire blossoms. Balaam's conflicting desire for his own, profitable way urges disagreement with God.

Modern-day "fees for divination" do not get tagged with such grotesque names. Their allurements are no less effective because of that, however. Whatever charm it is that insinuates itself into the range of the attention, capturing and holding it, becomes the "fee for divination." When this happens, the will of God becomes unwelcome in its limitations. How harsh it seems in its rigidity! It offers no choice, no alternative. "Go and make disciples of all nations" is just as clear as Balaam's "Do not go."

Delay is Balaam's next response to the revelation of God's will. Postponement obscures the rebellion of the heart from onlookers by cloaking it with an air of spirituality—I want to be absolutely sure of the Lord's will before I make a move. The inner anticipation is that delay will reveal an alternate way from God, that something will turn up that will relax the stringency of the demands of a conscience in which God is disturbing the peace.

But delay is disobedience. Why? Because delay means that God's basic requirement is being rejected now. Tomorrow's pledged obedience cannot be reckoned in today's account.

Blindness is the result of disagreement with God. In Balaam we see a man so blinded, in fact, that he cannot see what is plain to a donkey. Talk about a one-track mind! Circumstantial evidence shouts, "Stop!" But he pushes on. He can't be wrong—God has said he can go.

The trouble is that he has ignored God's condition—"If the men come to call thee . . ." (Num. 22:20, KJV). It is not recorded that they did; yet he moved off on his own. In this unhappy, relapsed state, he reacts to others in a mounting temper, the expression of his now crystallized self-centeredness. The poor donkey gets the brunt of it. Parents, pastors, friends all become the victimized donkeys of modern Balaams fighting God's way and rushing blindly into God's drawn sword.

Beware of being insistent with God. He may alter his word to allow you to go your way. But he has no alternate "good, pleasing and perfect will."

16

Our Role

Crusader or Ambassador?

A crusader is one who carries on an enterprise against real or supposed evils with great zeal. An ambassador is one sent on a special mission. It may seem uncalled-for to force a distinction between a crusader and an ambassador, for, after all, is there any defensible difference between the two roles? If so, then what does it matter, and to what degree? Is it important for a person to know that she has been sent by God, or is it enough for her to be involved in self-initiated service simply because she feels it is the right thing to do?

This question reaches down into fundamentals. Do we stir up our own hearts about the needs around us and then act? Or is there a reference point, higher than our hearts and feelings, to which we should orient ourselves and from which we should take our marching orders?

The story of Moses provides apt illustrations of both sides of this particular coin. Forty years of disillusionment followed Moses' initial attempt to serve his fellows. On the merely human level, the motivation that inspired Moses to be an activist for Israel was altogether commendable. Years of palace life had not erased from his mind the fact that the oppressed Israelite slaves were his people. In spite of circumstances, his loyalty was still to his own kith and kin, and ties of race and family called for involvement on their behalf. The dimension of his commitment at this stage was wholly out of proportion to the ultimate result. Sheer heroism was the mark of the man. Yet utter failure was stamped on what he did. In spite of good intentions, his effort climaxed in ignominy and issued in an aftermath of sour disappointment and crushed hopes.

The demeanor of Moses, the man that God wanted to send on his errands, was quite different. Confronted by God at the bush forty years later and faced with the fact that God was commissioning him to deliver the Israelites from Pharoah, how did he react? Was he glad for the opportunity to redeem a failure that had rankled through the years in the wilderness? Not at all. Instead he retreated into a hastily constructed refuge of refusals. One after another, he drove in the stakes to fence himself off from God's commission. Who am I? Who are you? They won't believe me. I'm not qualified. No way! Send whom you want, but don't send me! He was not about to tangle with the problem of delivering Israel again, resisting even to the point of angering God. Look at the public-spirited hero now. See how he has shrunk into a narrow-souled egoist. How the mighty are fallen!

The goal Moses had set for himself was to deliver Israel. The purpose God had in sending Moses was also to deliver Israel. The difference was not in the objective of the goal, but with Moses. He burned with zeal to go on his own terms, but he froze up when God wanted to send him. As a crusader, he had a cause. He was concerned for his people and what he planned to do for them, sure that God would be pleased with his contribution. He had no thought other than that the people would rally around him and then that Pharoah would quail before him.

Moses had to learn that inner steam generated by strong sympathies and worthy motives is ineffective in the accomplishing of God's will, even though its eruptive forces may honestly seek to do God's will. In fact, what he conceived to be God's will was probably confirmed to him in the unlooked-for opportunity to deal a smashing blow for the cause by bumping off an officious Egyptian.

But the end of such self-initiated action is entirely predictable, B.C. or A.D. The natural man will not accept the fact that "every natural virtue is death branded" (Oswald Chambers). God doesn't add his blessing to special efforts carried out by natural resources, but rather subtracts. He has to, or he wouldn't be God. Nor will he allow us to lean on the arm of our natural or acquired qualifications, even though he himself engineered our life circumstances to give us these advantages. To ignore this fact will lead us to a satirical anticlimax—a grave in the sand and a disillusioned man heading off into the wilderness.

The later success of Moses, however, in carrying out the greatest administrative feat the world has seen has its secrets. These are laid bare as lessons for us:

The biological fact of a birth can have profound theological significance. Like Moses, we are born when God's time is ripe. Like Esther, we come to royal position "for such a time as this." Like Jeremiah, we are ordained and set apart for our ministry before birth.

God engineers life circumstances for his chosen one to insure that no necessary equipment is lacking for the task he has in mind. Only God could work the miracle of arranging free education to the highest possible level for a man born in slavery.

The training God gives has no intrinsic value for spiritual work apart from God's direct control. (Unfortunately, the trained person is often the last one to believe this.)

The crusaders attempting great things under their own steam come up with nothing. They lack the touch of authority. The same people, when yielded to God and as his ambassadors, accomplish the impossible.

17

Faith's Alternate

Giving God Room Not to Deliver

There will always be times in life when the expectations of our faith will not be realized in the way we anticipated. For example, a young person fired with zeal to serve God applies for service overseas and is turned down by the mission board. Or a young couple, in love and convinced that the Lord wants them together, happily plan for their marriage. A war comes along, knocking the bottom out of their starry world. (I speak from experience on both counts.) Situations such as these and a hundred and one others quickly show how faith's confident expectations can be ruthlessly contradicted.

The book of Daniel introduces us to three men—Hananiah, Mishael, and Azariah. (By the way, I wish we could get these names into our heads instead of Shadrach, Meshach, and Abednego, the names with which pagan victors had tagged these men to expunge the significance of God from the names their families had given them.) The decree of Nebuchadnezzar that all people must bow to his image or burn in his fire brought these three men into prominence. Because they would not comply with the command, they incurred the wrath of this powerful monarch and faced a horrible death. The three heroes simply refused to consider the fire as a factor, turning rather to look to God and the spiritual resources available to them.

The stark, cold-blooded courage of Hananiah, Mishael, and Azariah as they faced the frothing fury of Nebuchadnezzar has always been a puzzle to the world—but not to the Christian who grasps the reality of God and the spiritual springs of his Word. With their backs to the wall, Daniel's three friends calmly gave their testimony of faith, expressed in two strong positives and an alternate: "The God we serve is able to save us from it, and he will rescue us. . . . But even if he does not . . . we will not serve your gods or worship the image of gold you have set up" (Dan. 3:17-18).

Faith's alternate, introduced by the words, "But if not," is no less an expression of faith than the two previous assertions. It gives, in fact, a demonstration of the reality of the faith the three men professed. In no way were they qualifying their statement to weaken the force of faith's first claims. Far from it. By adding to that testimony an opportunity for him to take another course for achieving his glory at their expense, they were giving it a new dimension.

Just suppose for a minute that Hananiah, Mishael, and Azariah had stopped after claiming, "Our God will deliver us," and that God had responded to their demand and kept them from the fiery furnace. They would have been saved, but the king's heart would not have been changed. There would have been no public acclamation of God as the great God of deliverances. God's superiority might not have been attested, and the three men would have missed the presence of the one "like a son of the gods" sharing the fire with them.

Furthermore, think of the example these men set for all the people through the ages who have faced torture and death for their faith. In giving expression to their defiant "But if not," the Hebrew exiles were insisting that mere physical deliverance from the cruel crunch of circumstances is less important than God's right to dispose of them according to his will.

An escapist generation reads security, prosperity, and physical well-being as evidences of God's blessing. Thus when he puts suffering and affliction into our hands, we misread his signals and misinterpret his intentions.

The prod to escape from situations we are afraid of comes from Satan. Peter urged the Lord Jesus to skip the sufferings of the cross. Yet to have yielded to the temptation would have robbed God of his victory weapon—the very weapon he had planned to be used in crushing the serpent's head. In turning to Peter with his "Get behind me, Satan," Jesus showed that he was well aware of the temptation's source.

Faith's alternative is that deep primary motivation that relates earth's afflictions to the word and will of God on one hand, and to his sovereign right to work for his glory in his own way on the other. Hananiah, Mishael, and Azariah understood God's command, "You shall not bow down. . . ." Because the command was clear, they looked for no compromise, in spite of Nebuchadnezzar's threat.

God doesn't supply cushions with his commands. If every command has to have a promise of deliverance to cushion the rugged absolute quality of its implications, God would be deprived of the powerful testimony of a faith that refuses to bend at the decree of any tyrant.

Pastor Wang Ming-tao of Peking asked for no cushion when he was put under pressure to compromise. This was his testimony: "As I obey the Lord whom I have served and as I keep the truth which I have believed, I will not obey any man's command that goes against the will of God. I have prepared myself to pay any price and make any sacrifice, but I will not change the decision I have made."*

Much of our Christian enterprise has lacked this significant note. C.H. Nash puts it this way:

> In the face of the appalling happenings of the present day we are being steadily compelled to realize that only through a fresh baptism of sufferings can the church be purged and fitted for the task which still confronts it in the evangelization of the non-Christian world. . . . The decisive battle of Christian truth . . . is yet to be fought. The enemy confronting the church will be armed with every kind of destructive device which human ingenuity can invent and diabolical subtlety devise; against which assaults the church will have nothing to present but the bared and helpless breast of suffering, and then it will be seen that ultimate victory lies with the weakest and not with the strongest.
>
> There is a call then for recruits in the army of the Lord who are prepared to enter the school of discipline

*Quoted from *Three of China's Mighty Men* by Leslie Lyall. (London: OMF Books, 1973).

and to give their lives without reserve to the exemplification of those ideals which our Master himself put to the fullest proof and by which he overcame the world.

What we see as God's recklessness is his way of putting into human hands an instrument of victory that he has carefully chosen and wondrously shaped for defeating the enemy and bringing glory to his name. God's way may seem to be the hard way, but it is the winning way.

18

Total toward Him

Directional Living

A TV commercial urges viewers to eat the complete breakfast cereal called Total. A Christian bookstore announces a new title on the woman's role in the church, *The Total Woman*. A newspaper from Asia claims that such-and-such should be a "total experience." In each context the word *total* starts a trend of thinking. A generation subjected to this emphasis comes to feel that business, industry, the church, or cultural and political patterns have conspired to block the road to their "total experience." But the protest voiced is always according to the individual's personal opinion as to what comprises "total."

Who is there to lift a voice against those who are willfully or ignorantly hacking great chunks off *God's* image of "total?" The prophet Hanani denounces Judah's King Asa for forsaking his earlier trust in God to call in help from the king of Syria and adds: "For the eyes of the LORD range throughout the earth to strengthen those whose hearts are fully committed [total] to him" (2 Chron. 16:9). Victory comes to the work and warfare of the Lord when his eyes, which are ceaselessly searching, spot someone whose heart is "total" toward him. And, conversely, defeat and disgrace dog the heels of the person who, like Asa, departs from total dependence on God to fill up his own idea of being total, doing his thing in his own way. God can freely use only the one who is total toward him.

The implication in the word *total* is that every necessary ingredient has been carefully sought out and included in the product. Thus if we transfer the thought to being *total toward God,* it will be necessary to study carefully the standards God has laid down, and then with diligence and discipline apply those standards to our living.

As I see it, the test of the total missionary is directional. Does she live toward herself or toward God and others? From start to finish the direction of our Lord Jesus' living and being was habitually outward. He went out from the glories of heaven and all the privileges that were his by right and, emptying himself of his rights, chose instead to assume responsibilities. Isaac Watts says it this way, "Love asks not, Must I give? but, May I sacrifice?"

Christ's example of true love in action has shown us what a total missionary essentially is. His kind of love not only took him outside of himself; it kept him out living and working in the interests of others. From his outside vantage point, he deliberately shut and locked the door, relinquished the key for others to claim by faith, and then nailed up a sign, "All rights and privileges resigned"—signed, "The Lamb of God."

Men could hound God's Son out of their cities and towns. They could shut him out of his world. But they could not drive him to seek a nest or a foxhole for his own comfort and safety inside that locked door. This directional living, always out toward others, defines what it means to be a total missionary. The concept may outrage us, but it is what being a total missionary is all about.

Our Lord develops this outward aspect in the parable he told of the three friends in Luke 11:5-8. The purpose of the parable is to teach us how to pray. The focus is sharpened on the man in the middle, the man who links his friend in need with another one who has the resources to meet that need. This man in the middle is the total missionary. From his example we are to learn how to pray and why he prays—so watch him.

The two things that drive him are, first, his sense of debtorship and, second, his dependence on someone else's resources. These make it imperative for him to do one thing—to ask. The obligation burdens him, but so does the fact that he has nothing wherewith to meet his obligation. Determinately, therefore, he presses on through midnight gloom to place himself in dependence on his friend in bed, and to batter and bang on the door until his friend is willing to respond and give him the bread he must have.

Putting the needs of others first and discrediting our own resources makes a good start for the servant of God, though these of themselves cannot bear fruit. The fruit is produced by the importunity in the man's asking.

But Jesus also has a word for those who would try to give less than total. He says, "With the measure you use, it will be measured to you" (Matt. 7:2). His life, his obedience, his dependence were all given without measure. His commitment was total. So the Father gave the Spirit without measure to him, and this factor made such giving possible. Our case is vastly different:

- Like Ananias, we measure the sacrifice and then try to justify a little trickery to avoid having to make the sacrifice total.

- Like Saul, we measure obedience by our own standards of convenience and then try to kid God that we have made it total.

- Like the scribe who said, "Lord, I will follow wherever you go," we want to make our professions of dedication bold and impressive. But we are easily turned aside when we discover that there is no nest or foxhole for the total missionary.

"One of the greatest needs of our modern Christian life," says Dr. J. Stuart Holden, "is that of recovering the sense of obligation to wholeheartedness [being total], which seems to be largely lost."

19

Candidate for Dying

Choosing Christ's Way

One of the qualifications of the servant of God that Paul lists for us is a real shocker. It jolts the spirit of the world that lurks in every one of us by the very starkness of its contrast. In a world that thinks so much of living and increasing the comforts and securities of that living, the idea of always carrying around "in the body the dying of the Lord Jesus" (2 Cor. 4:10, KJV) is obnoxious, repulsive, mystical, and altogether impractical.

This "dying of the Lord Jesus" is distinct from his actual death, even as the process is different from the climax. Dying was the process of his thirty-three years, and physical death the climax. The process started with his step out of heaven and his stoop to the cradle in Bethlehem's caravansary, and culminated at Calvary. His life was consistently a process of dying. In willing submission to the process he qualified for the redemptive climax, which was his death on the cross for the sins of the world.

You may be wondering how and where this dying is seen in the Gospel record in our Lord's life. It is seen in his unrelenting refusal to submit his living to the dictates of worldly wisdom, whether in the wilderness, on the Caesarea Philippi road, under Gethsemane's olive trees, or even on the cross. He died to the world's standards and value system for living. Neither the thinking of the world, nor his own promptings, impulses, or appetites moved him to action. He clung tenaciously to his "aliveness" in his Father, even as he refused to live as a self-propelled operator. His way was his dying. In the wilderness, hunger pangs agonizingly tempted him to cling to living and at the same time tested the depth and reality of his dying.

On the road to Caesarea Philippi, the temptation to spare himself the dying was all the more subtle in that it came from the lips of a loved disciple. But the well-intentioned Peter, vocalizing for the devil, called down on his own head the stern rebuke of the Savior: "Get behind me, Satan! . . . You do not have in mind the things of God, but the things of men" (Mark 8:33). To Jesus "the things of God" included the acceptance of what men would count as failure and shame. "The things of men" embrace success and security, and this mind is to be found even in the discipleship circle—and let us not limit this circle to Peter, James, and John.

Finally, when Jesus was on the cross, the chief priests and scribes called on him to come down from the cross and save himself. But save himself he would not; he clung to his dying.

The world equates "living" with the freedom of the individual to control his or her own affairs and the right to be considered as a person, to have his own way, or to do her own thing. "The dying of the Lord Jesus" was his refusal to insist on any of those rights. He accepted the injustices, the hating, the shaming as part of the redemptive process.

- He was Prince of life; yet he willingly yielded to dying.

- He was Lord; yet having accepted dying to self's rights as a way of life, he became servant to all.

- He was Creator of all, yet accepted the role of a carpenter in Nazareth.

- He alone was perfect; yet he refused to vindicate himself, and died as a criminal.

- He covered his success stories and exposed himself as an utter failure.

- He could have lived by calling in twelve legions of angels to protect himself, but he wouldn't even allow one sword to be used in his defense.

Jesus was a candidate for dying, where we, in contrast, are reluctant to think about daily dying. Our rights are more important than our responsibilities. We clutch hysterically to living, and feel threatened when God touches us at some point in our living. What bundles of contradiction we are! We are at once devoted to God and his cause and yet so very self-centered, a coexistence that his example and precept repudiates.

O Lord, if living means to me only a self-made life, insistence on my rights, and the satisfying of my hunger, then take me into your candidate school to learn of you and how to carry about in my body your dying.

20

Opportunity Price Tag

Repudiating Self's Claims

Opportunity for us as Christians is not just a collection of assorted goodies set before us to drool over while we try to decide which one we really want. Avowedly people want to serve the Lord, to know his will. Yet, when it comes to making a selection for service, personal preference rather than principle often influences the choice. Perhaps the main reason, at least for many of God's children, is ignorance of the principles that ought to be in operation in service opportunity selection.

As a commodity in God's market, opportunity is spiritual in content, even though it has very practical and personal implications. The danger comes when we allow the practical considerations to submerge spiritual content.

As a market commodity, opportunity comes with a price tag. In the States or Canada or anywhere in the free world, it might take a bit of time and effort, even courage, to buy up God's opportunity. But in China, Cuba, or Iran, where the price is subject to wild inflation, it could cost all that a man has to take a stand for his faith and to bear witness to Jesus Christ. And let's not kid ourselves that the price will decline if we stay out of the market. In these inflationary times, all indications point to a rising cost in the price of opportunity. Détente is but the expression of our wishful but unrealistic thinking. In the sinuous silk glove hides the iron hand.

In leading Christians to redemptive opportunities, Jesus Christ doesn't pander to the tastes of the natural human being. He doesn't sugar-coat his opportunities and then dangle them in front of us to lure us on. All opportunities on his list have a fixed price—sacrifice. They are available to those who are willing repudiate self's claims.

Some time ago a would-be missionary came to me with this question: "Would it be possible for you to arrange for me to be sent where the Communists won't come?" He was wanting to fit the opportunity for preaching the gospel into the limited circumference of his personal security. If we could arrange this for him, he would be in the market—otherwise not at all. He had yet to learn that God's price is fixed and that he was bankrupt of the currency God asks in exchange for his opportunity.

Teenager Daniel and his three friends, trudging wearily across the desolate wastes toward Babylon as Nebuchadnezzar's captives, could have argued that all opportunity for serving God was over as far as they were concerned. And who would have blamed them? Deported out of the land of their fathers by a cruel tyrant, torn from comfortable homes and separated from loved ones, surely they were facing the end of opportunity. Nothing could have looked less like an open door for life service than captivity in Babylon.

For decades Christians in China or Eastern Europe have faced a comparable situation in the accusations, arrests, and exiles that they have endured for Christ's sake. They, too, could have pleaded that the door was closed and their opportunity to serve the Lord over. Though many have paid the price demanded, no doubt many looked at the price tag even as they did in Daniel's day and lost interest in involvement for God.

It is time we sought God's definition of a closed door and forgot some of our own. When we hear the wolves howling, we think we have to rush for cover, lest we get hurt. Jesus saw things the other way. He said to his disciples, "I am sending you out like sheep among wolves." We are not justified in arguing that a door is closed just because danger is threatening.

Paul's reasoning endorses the Savior's remarks. He says to make "the most of every opportunity, because the days are evil" (Eph. 5:16). It was this that gave Watchman Nee his text when he returned to Shanghai under the communists in 1949, and found many of his friends preparing to escape. He himself was outside China at the time of Mao's takeover and could have stayed in the free world if he had heeded the advice of his friends. But through prayer God had showed him that his responsibilities lay in China. Daniel was taken captive to his assignment—he had no choice as to place. Watchman Nee was captive in another sense as he declared his intentions of going back into the "lions' den" of China.

We need to see that the captivity of Israel in Babylon had two sides. God's judgment on Israel's sin did not so dominate his thoughts that all other concerns were forgotten. Love precedes wrath, and the saving of people takes precedence over the punishing of people. God is redemptive before he is punitive. His Lamb submits meekly to being sacrificed on the altar before he rides forth to judge and make war. God's love sent Jonah to Nineveh and placed Daniel in Babylon. God coupled his mercy to Babylon with his punishment of Israel. What seemed a closed door in Babylon was only closed to those who rejected the price tag of God's opportunity. The door in China or Pakistan or Cambodia is closed only to those who are not willing to pay the price of making an opportunity.

Daniel and his three friends were placed where God wanted them, but it was up to them to make the opportunity for God. By purposing in their hearts not to yield one iota in their God-inspired convictions, they burst open the door of opportunity in a closed land. The faithful captives brought the tyrant dictator to his face before them, confessing, "Surely your God is the God of gods and the Lord of kings . . ." (Dan. 2:47). The price tag on this opportunity was: don't bow, but burn; don't give in, get thrown in! They bought it. The prisons and labor camps of China's bitter northwest are mute testimony to a similar faithful witness that the gospel's enemies have been unable to silence. No door is closed where men and women are prepared to cling to their convictions and refuse to be conformed to the squeeze of the world.

21

Time and the Towel

Rights vs. Responsibility

Life's most inexorable and inelastic commodity is time. We can hoard our pennies in a piggy bank, but we cannot stretch or shrink the ticking of the seconds on the time clock any more than we can halt the lengthening of the shadows as they reach across the field at sunset. We have no power to create or to manipulate the stream of time; all we can do is to navigate our little ship in its current.

When Jesus Christ lived on earth as a man, he was bound by time's limitations just as we are. His own statements proclaim his awareness of this limitation. Early in his ministry he says, "The right time for me has not yet come" (John 7:6). By the time we reach the account in John 13 of the washing of the disciples' feet, our attention is directed to Jesus' consciousness that his time is running out. John, in fact, roots his record of the Last Supper in this awareness with the words, "Jesus knew that the time had come for him to leave this world" (John 13:1). We are thus forced to conclude that this was dominant in Jesus' thinking, that he was realizing that his most limited resource as he gathered his disciples into the upper room was the element we call time. He was entering the last, unstretchable opportunity to complete the training the disciples needed to qualify for the work he had for them to do after his departure.

But time was not the only factor with which Jesus was concerned. Continuing the account, John writes, "Jesus knew that the Father had put all things under his power" (13:3). For Jesus that knowledge spelled accountability. He knew that the Father had committed to him the authority and responsibility for completing the work of salvation for a lost world; not only that, but also for making provision that the finished work be proclaimed in every land and to every creature.

The little band sitting around him in the upper room had been chosen in order that he might send them forth as his witnesses. Thus the special burden on his heart on this occasion related to their fitness for this strategic ministry. They must be made to understand not only their role in God's plan, but the qualifications needed to fulfill that role.

The fact that the account springs out of the sensitivity of Jesus to the limit of his opportunity with them is an indicator of the seriousness with which he regarded the situation. This deep concern was not without good reason—for we are soon made aware of the fact that the disciples were all sitting down to eat with dirty feet.

While failing to see that feet were washed may have been but a minor breach of cultural etiquette, I'm sure that during the meal it was far from a minor problem. The dirty feet revealed all too well a disturbing attitude among the disciples. As each man had entered the room, he was aware that someone ought to be going after a basin and a towel.

Yet not one of them had been able to bring himself to do this menial service for his fellows. How this must have distressed Jesus as he looked ahead to the larger task he was about to commit into their hands.

Why? First, the disciples had a wrong attitude to time and opportunity. Each uncomfortably tried to close his eyes to the responsibility of washing dirty feet, hoping that by procrastinating, something would happen that would take the need for action out of his hands.

There are two ways of looking at time. Either it is a precious opportunity to be bought up, or it is as unwanted as the guest who hangs around and will not go home. Jesus was watching the clock to make sure that he did not miss the opportunity. The disciples were watching and hoping that the time would run out to end the opportunity.

It was this attitude of the disciples toward the opportunity that Jesus knew he would have to correct. The evangelization of the world would never be carried through by men who procrastinated because their minds were on the last trumpet, not on the opportunity. To some Christians the lostness of the world is not the voice of opportunity; it is an unwelcome guest they hate to hear knocking at the door. It embarrasses them, and they reckon that if they pretend to be out, the opportunity will go away.

But the attitude of the disciples toward the clock was only a part of the problem. Sitting around the table, each was inwardly standing guard over his rights, ready to raise a storm should those rights be threatened.

Not one of the disciples was without a good reason why someone else should do the servant's job. Peter would argue that he was the leader of the group. James already had his eye on the seat at the right hand of the throne whenever Jesus should set up his kingdom. John felt that he was closest to the Master and was therefore obliged to stick close to him. And Judas, of course, would object to any addition to his quota of responsibility as treasurer.

How could Jesus leave his work in the hands of men so lacking in the spirit of willingness to sacrifice their rights in order to fulfill their responsibilities? The world would never be evangelized—and will not be today—as long as God's chosen servants are concerned first with their own rights. So Jesus shows the disciples by example how to treat their rights. His act in taking a towel, getting a basin of water, and then washing their feet was his way of saying that personal rights have no place when God's opportunity is knocking on the door.

The passion of Jesus' kind of Christianity is manifested by a deliberate signing away of our rights in order to become his bondservants. Our only right as his followers is to give up our rights.

Surely this incident throws a searching question at today's church: How much of the undone in the as-yet-unfinished task of world evangelism is because we have adopted the world's priority of rights over responsibilities?

22

Wrestling

When Satan Invades Culture

Our generation has eyed with increasing trepidation the successive waves of evil-slanted phenomena that have infiltrated the human stream. The central influences of life are being invaded. We are under attack. Drugs that blow the mind have taken captive a sizable slice of the upcoming generation. Others are caught up with music deviations that overpower the emotion-control centers. On the moral scene, permissiveness blurs issues and weakens the will to resist. With many people accepting this as a way of life, the moral fiber that is the strength of a people is being rotted. Enemy attack has reached every part of our corporate being—physical, mental, moral, and spiritual. The pattern in all of these aberrations is slanted toward breaking away from God.

In other words, the rulers and authorities in the heavenly realms have rigged their Trojan horse, infiltrated through society's defenses, and opened the gates for a flood of evil to take over. Scripture would have us be aware that supernatural evil powers can and do establish themselves in local culture and dominate life and custom.

In the book of Revelation, the messenger of the church in Pergamum is reminded that he dwells "where Satan has his throne" (Rev. 2:13). The obvious implication is that Satan's infiltration had reached its intended conclusion in the establishing of a center of authority. From this point the leader of the evil forces is able to direct and control the opposition to God's purposes of grace.

Questions flood into our minds. How do the "rulers and authorities" erupt into the human stream? Can we control and prevent their intrusion? Or are we to sit, passive and aloof, watching and wringing our hands while the enemy enters and plays havoc with society's foundations? There must be something we can and should be doing.

But what is that something, and how do we go about it? Listening to good sermons in church or on the radio or TV might bring personal edification, but does not touch the problem. Praying for our missionaries and the sick is our responsibility—but having done it, we are still bound to say, "We have left undone that which we ought to have done."

Paul urges us to "stand against the devil's schemes," meaning that the individual believer and the local corporate body of believers are to place themselves at that vantage point that will best stop enemy incursions. James says, "Resist the devil, and he will flee from you," enjoining us to active opposition to the devil. We dare not ignore this teaching and remain spectators on the sidelines. The call to battle must be sounded where the enemy infiltration is spotted, then the defenses manned and our attacking forces armed and deployed to oppose the enemy and to drive him away.

I read Paul's words, "we wrestle not . . ." (Eph. 6:12, KJV), and there I'm tempted to stop, to sigh and mutter, "How true!" Wrestling is the most unpopular activity in the church today. We praise, petition, supplicate, intercede— but we do not wrestle.

Actually we do wrestle. But it is with God over our own trials. That obviously is not what Paul means when he says, "we wrestle not against flesh and blood . . ." The emphasis is on a contrast that he is about to introduce.

There were indeed flesh-and-blood enemies that opposed Paul in his ministry. Luke describes the campaign in Ephesus in Acts 19, and it is reasonable to infer that in writing to the Ephesian church about his wrestling, Paul is thinking of the events reported in that chapter. He would remember the incidents involving the seven sons of Sceva from the hippie Jewish sect, who practiced the occult, and Demetrius, the silversmith. These were the "flesh and blood."

But Paul realized that men who opposed him were but instruments controlled by non-flesh-and-blood supernatural powers. Having entered the human stream through the local culture, these powers were expressing their hate and opposition to God and his servants in the cultural customs of occultism and Diana worship. So Paul asserts that he wasn't tangling with the culture itself or the men dominated by it, but—and here comes the contrast—against "rulers, against the authorities, against the powers of this dark world and against the spiritual forces of evil in the heavenly realms" (Eph. 6:12).

These supernatural powers, arrayed under hell's imperial majesty, formed the target for his wrestling. When these controlling powers were broken by Paul's wrestling above and beyond them, flesh-and-blood people were persuaded to burn fifty thousand pieces of silver's worth of their books on the occult.

With Timothy or Erastus as his "Aaron and Hur," Paul had climbed above the puppets on the streets to assert the authority in heavenly places of the church's Head over Satan and all his power. Though pressed out of measure and above strength, Paul and his band stood, and, having overcome all, continued to stand. Their wrestling may have upset the anthropologists of Paul's day, but it disclosed an abiding and effective secret in church growth that we dare not ignore as we face the same supernatural powers and similar cultural aberrations today.

23

Sent to Reap

Gleaning Is for Paupers

In a world ready for reaping, who will do the reaping, and who the gleaning? Dedication is strong on the side of communism, the forces of revolution, and the purveyors of false religion and moral permissiveness. The enemies of Christ have their eyes on the harvest and make this their priority. With them all activity contributes to one goal.

The church, on the other hand—not sure of the uniqueness of Christ and confused over priorities—is losing its reaper role in the harvest field. Competitive bickering, characteristic of the gleaner role, marks the attitude of many of its members. Those who call themselves Christ's friends sometimes become too fussily defensive of the definition of evangelicalism to have time for evangelism. The hands that should be wielding sickles have lost their appointed role and have substituted a meaner one, that of picking up the leftovers while pushing and shoving others who are reaching after the same mean handfuls.

Gleaning and reaping are quite distinct from each other. Gleaning was God's welfare scheme to insure that the poor would be provided for. It was his arrangement for society's unfortunates and misfits. Whatever gleaning means in spiritual terms, it does not represent a divinely appointed vocation. While God has made provision for the spiritually impoverished, he neither chooses anyone nor appoints anyone to glean.

The gleaner's life in ancient Israel was at the lowest level in society—the level where restlessness and anxiety prevailed. In itself, gleaning offered no way up to a higher strata. As a job it provided minimum satisfaction with maximum worry.

Gleaning is competitive, not cooperative. The pangs of hunger and the grim specter of starvation spurred the ancient gleaner to savage rivalry. The picture is not true unless it includes the idea of one desperate beggar contesting with other desperate beggars.

Gleaning is self-initiated toil, uncontrolled and uncommanded as to field or time. Jesus does not command, Go into all the world and glean what the Communists or Buddhists have dropped. The command Jesus gave was, "I sent you to reap" (John 4:38). The service of God is never meant to be self-initiated scavenging.

Gleaning is carried on in the right place, but with the wrong motivation. The supply is there, but the rights of the gleaner are restricted to the leftovers. Where is fulfillment in a life lived at the gleaner level?

Gleaning pictures life with a handicap, a life overshadowed with anxiety and bitter with jealousy. It represents life restricted, subnormal, and self-centered.

On the other side of the coin, let's look at the reaper. A reaper is not left to his own devices. In the harvest field of the world God makes his appointments as Lord of the harvest. His reaper-appointees are sent out on the employer/employee basis—"the reaper draws his wages," says the Scripture. The reaper has an honorable and rewarding vocation.

Jesus asserts that reaping for God is priority business. He would have us "ask the Lord of the harvest, therefore, to send out workers into his harvest field" (Matt. 9:38). This is his command. It is important that the harvest be reaped for God and not left for enemies to capture—for harvests not gathered when they are ripe are either reaped by others for their own ends or left to perish. It is this that creates the emergency.

Reaping is the key to history. When the harvest is gathered, the end comes and the curtain falls—not the Bamboo or Iron Curtain, but the curtain of God's final act of sealing up affairs in the world's harvest.

What ought to concern us is that while the church is preoccupied with other things, the enemies of Christ are out in full force to reap the harvest. Materialism has replaced Mao as the new cult of China's millions. Buddhism in various countries is putting on a new face to win new allegiance. Islam claims that soon her symbol of crescent moon and star will supplant the Christian's cross. Mormons, liberals, and representatives of all sorts of sects and heresies are busy with sharpened sickles. Harvests ripe today are lost to God tomorrow. His priority workers, therefore, must be reapers. Can we consider acceptable to him any service that does not contribute in some way to reaping that which will otherwise be lost?

24

The "Now" Factor

The Dual Application

Most of us are familiar with the annual missionary conference in our churches. The main emphasis has been to justify missionary enterprise from biblical grounds and to assert the validity for involvement beyond the local to include "every creature." But one important factor is often overlooked or underemphasized. We lay on our people their obligation to become involved, but fail to insist that the action be now. God's set time for decision and moral action is immediate, for "now is the acceptable time."

We have limited the "now" to the lost person's need to respond in repentance to God's offer of reconciliation, and have failed to see a dual application.

If the acceptable time for the sinner to turn to God is now, then it stands to reason that the acceptable time for preaching the gospel is now. We are tough on the poor sinner who wants to procrastinate, to take time to think it over. Yet the Christian has only to say, "I don't believe it is God's will for me to get involved now," and we let him get away with it. We must witness now if men are to accept now.

When Paul was talking about "the acceptable time" (2 Cor. 6:2, NASB), he was quoting from Isaiah 49. He knew this passage well. Twice he quotes from it. In one of Paul's readings of this chapter, the Holy Spirit had flashed new light on its significance. Isaiah 49:6, "I will also make you a light for the Gentiles that you may bring my salvation to the ends of the earth," had previously pointed him to the coming Messiah, the servant of Jehovah. But the Holy Spirit in Paul's heart was now widening the application. We have our inner quarrels with those who pick out obscure verses from the Old Testament and claim guidance from them. Yet that is just what Paul does here. He takes this verse as God's command to him. He bases his claim to be the apostle to the Gentiles on this verse, stating, "For this is what the Lord has commanded us" (Acts 13:47).

"The acceptable time" that we preach at the sinner applies equally to those who are commanded to be God's salvation to the ends of the earth. Now is the time to preach. A biblical view of missions requires emphasis on now/action.

Periodically some congress on missions will sound a catch phrase such as "The evangelization of the world in this generation!" Yet even this conditions this generation to faulty thinking on the time factor. It was to counter this kind of approach that Jesus said, "Do you not say, 'Four months more and then the harvest'? I tell you, open your eyes and look . . ." (John 4:35). He would not have us count on any time other than now. We are not entitled to the right to set time goals for God's work. Jesus would say to us, "Don't go setting harvest goals that will rob you of initiative to act now, for now is the day for salvation to be preached."

Any second volume to the book of Acts will never be written as a result of careful plans that postpone the harvest until four months or four years of discussions, research, and preparation are complete. The Holy Spirit moves in power along lines he has established and in accordance with his own predetermined and prestated time factor. That time factor has never been anything else but now—for people must hear now.

One cardinal evil the devil uses to tempt us is the delusion that we will gain something by procrastination. We allow ourselves to be deluded into thinking that our time for involvement is when we have finished training, when we have done our research, after we have been able to get organized. All this presupposes that we have available time, be it four months or a generation. Jesus warned time-conscious disciples, "It is not for you to know the times or dates the Father has set" (Acts 1:7).

The word the church has for the world is *today*. And the word that God has for the church is also *today*. The church needs a "now" re-generation in her thinking!

I am not against planning, training, or research. But these things should never be allowed to weaken the obligation of the church's "now" involvement in the work of the Holy Spirit.

25

When We Are "De-elected"

Focusing on God's Sovereignty

The sandy-haired young man stood dumbfounded. He had applied to the Peace Corps and had been called in for orientation and training. Now the letter in his hand was headed "De-election Notification." The door to the Peace Corps had slammed in his face.

De-elected. Rejected. A dead end. Where does the young man go from here?

In the Midwest a Christian Education major fairly glows with the assurance that God is leading her along in his will, thrilled at what he is doing for her. With confidence she applies to a mission board. Weeks later, however, when a rejection letter arrives, the bottom of her world drops out, and gloom replaces the sunshine. What happened to her guidance? Where is God now?

What about those "white-envelope" experiences in our lives? Is de-election a spiritual principle of First Cause? Or does it happen that people can bungle something and upset the will of God for my life? The answer is important.

In finding our way in this, we need to look first at the basis of our assurance that we have been led of God. Guidance is more than my interpretation of what I think God is doing. Guidance is more than an unconnected thread. It is God moving and working by his Holy Spirit to produce a pattern of interweaving and contributing threads. The sense of being guided has to be the smallest part of what is happening; the fact of a sovereign Lord working all things together for good is the overriding consideration. It is on this fact that faith must concentrate.

Focusing on the sovereign working of God develops a pattern-consciousness instead of our too common one-thread consciousness. It helps me see that if God is leading me, then he must be leading others who have a bearing on my life. This gives me a cross-bearing so that I can check to see whether I am in his will or just deceiving myself.

Let's go back, then, to our original question: Can the decision of a person or even a group of people put me out of the will of God for my life? Are second causes in certain situations able to overrule the supreme First Cause, who, of course, is God? To admit that I am at the mercy of people and their very fallible judgments is tantamount to denying that God is omnipotent and that he works sovereignly in his creation to fulfill all that he has planned for each of his children.

We are not at the mercy of others, any more than Jesus was at the mercy of Herod, Pontius Pilate, and the mob at his trial. Scripture affirms that they were limited in their action to what God's "power and will had decided beforehand should happen" (Acts 4:28). God does use people to work out his purposes, and he sets limits to what they can do.

Take the case of Paul. He was ready for service—so he probably thought—but he was asked to go back home. The apostles served him a de-election notice. But in God's own time Paul was back on the front line. The explanation of what happens is God, his will, his power, his time; never is it that a mistake has been made.

The devil's masterpiece of subtlety is in getting us absorbed with what we have classified as a mistake. In this orbit we stew, we boil, we burn. We fail to see anything of God in what has happened to us, and we have no inclination to accept any affirmation that God is responsible for any part of what we are going through. The whole focus of thought is that somebody has made a mistake. I speak as one who has been through an experience of de-election, having been turned down when I made my first application to the China Inland Mission.

Often what really happens is that we magnify God's will for us above God himself. We almost worship at the altar of what God is doing in our lives. We allow the purpose to supersede that person, the plan to obscure the planner, and God's place in our hearts to be usurped. Then God, concerned for his throne rights in the heart, steps in and lets us feel a pressure from his hand, a pressure designed to draw us back to himself.

The way to victory in a situation like this lies in a positive reaffirmation from the ground of faith, that God is the sovereign cause for all that happens to his children. We will not straighten matters out by grappling with those who seem to have made the mistake or who have done the wrong thing. For the child of God things fall into place by the action of faith in the presence of God, a faith that refuses to be offended by what has happened and that accepts his orderings. The purpose in all that God does with us is that we might be made pliable in his hand and unresistant. To such is the promise, "The meek will he guide in judgment: and the meek will he teach his way" (Ps. 25:9, KJV).

26

Divine Designation

The Fire Must Not Go Out

The Israelite rabble, newly escaped from the clutches of proud Pharoah, needed time to develop their national consciousness and to establish their God as King in their new nation, and to become familiar with the constitution God gave them through Moses. So for a full month following the setting up of the tabernacle the Lord outlined the rituals and sacrifices recorded in Leviticus. God purposed to dwell among them, in their camps, and this wonderful fact was meant to establish the character of their life from this point on.

Then as we pass from the details of sacrifices and God's standards of holiness in Leviticus and start going through the book of Numbers, we are surprised by a dramatic shift. Suddenly we are introduced to God's Selective Service Act. God orders the numbering of Israel's men of war. Inherent in God's character is an aggressiveness against sin and a motivation to redeem mankind from its bondage.

But in order to wage war and to deliver captives, God needs men and women. If God's light is to shine in the world and to dispel its darkness, it will be through human light-holders. If his truth is to displace the lies and deceit of Satan, it will only be as men and women pay the price for holding to the truth and strive together for the spread of the gospel. If the knowledge of the one true and living God is to overthrow the worship of false gods, God needs demonstrators to display the transcendent glory of his grace and power. The purposes of God for his people do not end with the blessings of their deliverance from Egypt. The Lord needs them to fulfill a vital role in his warfare against all the power of the enemy.

In this move from ceremonies to the more practical facts of living, God is showing the development that is to characterize the life and service of the Christian. Salvation and the divine indwelling are the preliminary steps to the call for active service. Not many people seem to realize this; yet the picture that is given here should dispel any illusions about the character of the Christian life. It is a life of the drawn sword.

But as the registration of the men moves forward, God suddenly interrupts the proceedings with a special command: "You must not count the tribe of Levi"(Num. 1:49). The draft board was not to include this tribe in the census of Israel's fighting men.

Any who have the hot blood of patriotism flowing through their veins will have some idea of what it must have meant to the men of Levi to be set aside. The heroic always carries with it more romance than a mundane stay-at-home existence. What could be more important than fighting at the spearhead of attack for the cause of their God? And what could be more ignominious than having to stay at home and be de-elected, when their peers are sent out to fight for the homes and families of the nation? It must have been a blow to the pride of the men of Levi. Perhaps the patriotic spirit has died out, but I think you will understand something of what it must have meant to the men of Levi when they heard the decision that they were not to be included in the muster for war.

Obviously there is a lesson here on priorities. Was God disqualifying the men of Levi? Far from it. Nor would it be reasonable to suppose that he was giving them up for some unimportant, second-rate service. The truth is that he was singling them out as an elite corps of specialists to act as his royal guard, with a top-priority assignment. In fact, they were so important to him that, in a representative capacity, he claimed them for himself. "The Levites are to be mine," God declared. Theirs was a special task. They were "to stand before the Lord to minister and to pronounce blessings in his name." (Deut. 10:8).

Judah and the warriors of the other tribes might be out on the battlefield slugging it out with the Hittite, Amorite, Amalekite, or whomever—but the strength of their cause and the roots of their victory lay in the fact that their brethren, the men of Levi, were back at home, camped around God's tabernacle and keeping the fires burning on his altar of sacrifice. For had not God commanded, "The fire must be kept burning on the altar continuously; it must not go out" (Lev. 6:13)?

The importance of this service was such that to allow it to fall into disarray would immediately be reflected in a lack of success at the front line. The death or wounding of soldiers in battle is one of the expected hazards of war. But to let the altar fire go out and the sacrifices cease would create a hazard they could not afford to consider.

The place of God in the life of a people is always more important than the activities of the group. This is because spiritually productive activities stem from and are the result of God's being given his rightful place. Accorded his throne-rights in a group or in an individual, he will soon make it manifest where his priorities lie.

Draft boards can only exclude the disabled from the muster for war. But when God is in command, he can choose whom he will for his royal guard. These special ones do not come to their appointment as priests by default, but by deliberate divine designation. Therefore if God has set you apart for special priestly ministries, "do not be negligent now, for the LORD has chosen you to stand before him and serve him, to minister before him and to burn incense" (2 Chron. 29:11). You are God's gift to his great High Priest to offer prayer as incense, just as the Levites were given as a gift to Aaron and his sons, to keep the fires burning on the altar of God.

27

Living That Counts

Accepting Discipline, Accomplishing Mission

God has a plan for me. In the body of Christ I have a role to play, likely many roles. God purposes to use me, surely, in the lives of people he will bring across my path. But what is to keep me from stumbling haphazardly through the days, months, and years ahead and missing much of what God has planned for me? How can I ensure that I can someday look back and say as Jesus could, "I have complet[ed]the work you gave me to do" (John 17:4)?

What kind of a person can be expected to press through the accumulations of strain to finish his course well? Is there some character quality that will endure the pressures of life in God's place for a person?

We won't find the answer in philosophizing, but in the living experience of the Son of Man as he mixed with men in all the strains and antagonisms of fishbowl living. In the face of every kind of opposition and in all sorts of situations,

Jesus Christ was able at the end to report back to his heavenly Father, "Mission accomplished."

But complementary to Jesus' claim to having accomplished the Father's assignment was the comment of Scripture, "he learned obedience from what he suffered" (Heb. 5:8). Herein is our answer. Jesus accomplished his mission because he accepted the discipline required of him.

Paul speaks of the dying of the Lord Jesus. This is not so much in reference to his death as to the daily dying that characterized his life. He consistently resisted living for himself. Dying to the devil's lure of self-preservation, he refused to make bread for himself out of stones. Dying to the temptation of an easy way to the crown, he turned a deaf ear to the devil's plea that he throw himself down from the pinnacle of the temple. Jesus rebuked Peter's statement that Christ surely would not suffer and die, with a stern "Get behind me, Satan!" The treasure Jesus guarded was more than his life—it was his dying. To have relinquished the dying at any point in favor of some escape scheme would have forfeited for him the right to claim, "Mission accomplished."

Surely this principle applies to anyone who would follow Christ, for is not this just what he taught his disciples: "If anyone would come after me, he must deny himself and take up his cross and follow me"? The one who will be able to claim "Mission accomplished" is the one who accepts the daily discipline of dying, for he is choosing to renounce and repudiate the competitive voice of self.

Life is a two-sided affair. One side is idealistic, the other practical. A person's call to serve God in some specific way is in the area of the idealistic. At first it all seems vague and uncertain, but the conviction grows as the vision becomes clearer, until it finally masters us. At this point we bring our call, as we conceive it, down to the level of the practical and place it alongside our natural abilities and personal preferences. Then, if we are young, we adjust our education so that it may bring some useful contribution to the great ideal. As we settle down to become a linguist, nurse, doctor, or educator, or otherwise build our career, the goal ahead inspires us, and the fire within drives us. We press forward with zeal and conviction, impatient and intolerant of anything that threatens to impede our progress. At this stage mission is the important thing in life. And because the job has a cloud-nine spiritual aura about it, we poke our heads through into thin air, unconcerned about the merciless blunderings of our hot feet down on earth.

In other words, we live in one dimension and tend to forget or ignore the practical matter of relating life's high ideals to the business of ordinary living with all sorts of crazy people. When God sends his diciplines into our lives, things seem sometimes altogether twisted. Why does God have to mediate his disciplines through the clumsy and unsympathetic hands of those we dislike and despise and whose authority we resent? Granted, we need discipline— but why not through acceptable channels?

When we are suffering from spiritual myopia, in fact, we would like to ignore the discipline as unnecessary for us. Of course, it is needed for those who are not as far advanced spiritually as we are. Our vision is clear: we are ready for whatever lies ahead and are cocksure that we will not be one of those who fail. Thus by our attitude we deny God the chance to say of us, "he or she learned obedience."

God purposes to build into us a quality of endurance. He has selected as choice for his purpose the things we suffer at the hands of our fellow human beings. The process of adjusting to the vagaries of those we would in the natural world consign to awful places, mellows and matures character. The business of bearing about in our bodies the dying of the Lord Jesus is the way idealists have their visions transmuted into living that counts in the murky world of human relations.

The people who will stay with their assignments through thick and thin are the ones who carry this record: "Discipline accepted." These people are more concerned to guard their daily dying than their living rights. God's people are the ones who accept the daily dying because it is indispensable and an integral part of accomplishing their mission. If we want to be able to say down the road, "I have completed the work you gave me to do," let us welcome the incompatibilities that toughen spiritual temper and at the same time drive us to the resources of the life that was laid down for us.

28

Life's Impact

Measured by God's Ultimate

Supporters of missions or prison ministries or whatever are sensibly concerned about results. They want to know whether an organization's drum-beating can be validated by measurable impact. Thinking Christians are critically scrutinizing, not so much the sales pitch of a group, but whether organizations and methods are geared for results.

We look at the impact of our own lives and ministry as well. Sometimes *impact* is hardly the word, and not necessarily because we haven't tried or worked hard at making a difference in our world.

While overseas I was asked to speak at a conference on "The Impact of Missions in Southeast Asia." The subject stuck doggedly in my mind as I traveled from country to country. Impact? I kept thinking of *bang* or *crash*—or at least *splash*—in terms of our mission's accomplishments.

Then one day I was walking along a beautiful tropical beach on Mindoro Island in the Philippines. At the top of the beach was a stone sea wall. In the water were all sorts of juicy jellyfish. One still alert to boyish fancies, I immediately put jellyfish and wall together and got *splosh!*—impact! Thus when a bright young missionary asked me what I was going to speak on at the conference, I told her impishly: "The Futility of Trying to Breach a Stone Wall with Jellyfish."

But I was serious. Were we really making an impact on Asia? Had Japan's iron web of conflicting social loyalties softened to allow converts an easy escape from its toils under the preaching of God's Word? Had hardened souls in any numbers broken away from Chinese secret societies in Malaysia or Hong Kong? How did our successes stack up against atheistic communism? Against militant nationalism? Did our presence in Asia really pose a threat to Islam or the hold of animism?

Or was the score really stacking against us? Was it possible for mere missionary mortals to prevail to such a point as could be labeled *impact?* Were our efforts any more effective than jellyfish against a stone wall?

You may feel that same futility in your neighborhood, your office, among your relatives. Is success just a matter of method or heart? Or are there other principles involved?

We often meditate on the impact of the perfect life of Christ. It was a life lived to capacity in the power of the Holy Spirit, a life directed in word and act by God the Father. Yet that life was hounded to a dreadful cross and nailed there to die. What a shattering anticlimax to the impact expectations of his friends! "We had hoped that he was the one who was going to redeem Israel," they said despairingly.

Where was the kingdom? Where were the thrones? Had the obdurate walls of Judaistic tradition cracked or crumbled? Did the people rally to continue his program? Was the hostility of the Pharisees relaxed? The answers are not hard to find. Look at the masses as they add their voice to the senseless hate cries that are calling for his death. And these were the people he spent himself to help and heal. Watch as his own selected disciples forsake him and run as danger suddenly confronts them.

Did the mission of Jesus Christ make any impact at all on his generation? Had he pitched unnecessarily into something too implacable to make any appreciable dent? Was he naive in trusting in the power of obscure spiritual forces? Did he not only fail in his mission, but also let himself be shattered by the impact? The pragmatists would despise anyone giving literal values to the claims and commands of a leader thus so signally discredited.

But there is another word, a last word. For those interested in measuring the impact of his life, Jesus told the parable of the tenant farmers, who beat up and shamefully treated the landowner's servants and finally killed his son (Luke 20:9-18). The impact of these men's actions was temporary failure for the owner's mission. But read on. Having quoted from the Old Testament, "The stone the builders rejected has become the capstone," Jesus warned: "he on whom it falls will be crushed." Talk about impact and the last word! On which side is the victory now?

We learn that the impact of any given mission is to be measured not in the immediate circumstances of a given point of time, but at God's ultimate time. Why is this so? For the same reason we don't stand at the foot of Calvary's cross on Good Friday to bemoan the failure of Christ's life and the dissolution of his cause!

Suffer a word of testimony from a missionary or a believer who has been subjected to threats, hatred, and cruelty. I affirm that the apparent triumph of the oppressors in a local situation is so charged through with fear and unrest that all the satisfaction in their achievement is nullified. On the other hand, the despised Christian is led out of initial fears into deep peace and quiet assurance. You can never persuade me that God is using the wrong method to fulfill his mission. Through experience I have learned that some victory is in reality and in the end sheer failure and that, contrariwise, apparent failure is often ultimately solid victory.

29

Beyond Training

Building Focus Godward

Moses faced an assigment that so bristled with unsur-
mountable problems that no staff officer today in his or her
right mind would have tackled it. He was not only to launch
a large scale military operation, but he was to do it with a
horde of untrained people as manpower. Only the miracle-
working of God kept the undertaking from foundering.

Think a moment about the difficulties. Besides being
untrained, the 600,000 men Moses was to lead against the
Canaanites had their flocks and herds with them. More,
their very unmilitary and therefore not easily controlled
families were also tagging along to provide explosive potential for panic and mass hysteria in the event of sudden
trouble. And to crown this rising scale of debits, mixed in
their company was a group of hangers-on whose loyalty
was open to question. Talk about an impossibly clumsy
force of maximum unwieldiness!

The significance of all of this begins to become apparent only as we see this exodus operation as one designed by God and executed by the man of his choice. The purpose of God was twofold: one, the deliverance of this mass of people from the power of an unwilling, arrogant, and powerful Pharaoh; and, two, to lead these people through the heart of Sinai and to bring them fit to fight a war of conquest in Canaan, finally to plant his people in the land.

God's choice of a man through whom to fulfill his purpose was Moses. In the fire that burned in the bush God presented himself to Moses with the commission: "So now go, I am sending you . . ."

To this call is a background we cannot ignore. Forty years earlier Moses had moved to do the very thing God was asking him to do now—to deliver Israel from Pharaoh's bondage. At that time "it came into his heart to visit his brethren" (Acts 7:23, KJV). In the language of today this would read: "I feel that God has called me to do such and such." The desire was in Moses' heart and the training in his sheepskin. But for all his training, Moses had neither the authority nor the ability for God's specific service. His preparation was incomplete, as subsequent events proved.

The point is this: The desire of the heart to do God's will, together with the best training in the world, does not constitute the call of God.

In the case of Moses, two things didn't change over the forty years: one, the purpose of God to deliver his people and, two, his training qualifications for Moses. We dare not ignore the inscrutable fact that only God knows how much character-building preparation an individual needs over and above all he acquires from the world's seats of learning. It is quite probable that we, as Moses, are not as ready as we think we are for God to use us effectively. Miss Marie Monsen, a missionary God would eventually use to bring revival in parts of China, discovered this. She wrote: "I came home on my first furlough with an uneasy feeling that my first term of service had been spent mainly for my sake. . . ."

There is a difference between being trained in some field of learning and being prepared in heart. Moses was trained in all the education of Egypt but was totally unprepared in heart for God's mission through him. A trained person may be more inclined to say yes to his or her own plan than yes to God. A prepared person should say yes to any word of God and no to all that comes from self. For someone who is trained, status, education, and skill tend to be the center of focus. For a prepared person, the center of focus is God's will and way.

With training alone, Moses failed to achieve God's objective. But prepared by God, Moses was master of this tremendous exodus operation and under God carried it through.

Dare we predict when we are ready for any specific task? Dare we question the delays and the disciplines, treating them as mistakes that God ought to overrule? If I am in a guidance vacuum as Moses was for forty years, I must accept it that God has seen me as unprepared for what he has in mind for me in some aspect of his great mission. If I am exercised by the circumstance in an attitude of humble brokenness, then "light dawns for the upright," and I will be ready in his time to be used of him for any given task.

30

Divine Perspective

Storm Clouds As God's Chariots

In the natural mind our human perspective on current
events is low-centered. We tend to look at the circumstances of life in terms of what they may do to our cherished
hopes and convenience, and we shape our decisions and
reactions accordingly. When a problem threatens, we rush
to God, not to seek his perspective, but to ask him to deflect
the trouble. Our self-concern takes priority over whatever
it is that God might be trying to do through the trouble.
One of the harder lessons of life is to learn that our
low-centered, sense-oriented subjectivism militates against
our effective cooperation with God in his purpose for us in
a given trial.

In order to bring this point home to us, I want to introduce to you a Daniel you may not be too well acquainted
with. The teenage part of his life is generally skipped over
because of the interesting things that happened later.
Watch with this fourteen-year-old as the trumpet blast

alerts Jerusalem to the approach of Nebuchadnezzar's army, sending shivers down the boy's spine and setting the whole city agog with fear and confusion. Feel with him as cruel hands separate him from loved ones and herd him into the group destined for captivity. Walk with him in the captive train as soldiers prod him from his beloved country and across the weary, dusty miles to Babylon. With each step hope sinks lower, and physical discomforts sap his spiritual stamina. And then pray with him as he anticipates the ruthless pressures of monopolized life in a totalitarian state, without the accustomed religious props.

But how do you pray in a situation like this? What are you to pray for? What chance will there be of being any use to God or country as a captive in a heathen country? How do you pray when your storehouse of hope and promise is suddenly emptied, when the future turns into a dead-end street? How are you to confront God with the fact that your life potential and possible usefulness to him has just been canceled out?

Thousands of others besides Daniel have had to face similar situations. For them and for us Daniel provides a principle of response. It is the sort of circumstance that Daniel had to face that matures us and drives us to seek God, not just for our relief, but for his own sake. Let us see what the young captive has to say about this terrible situation that has befallen him and his people and about the mission of God in the world.

In verse one of the book of Daniel, he gives us the low-centered human perspective on the news—"In the third year of the reign of Jehoiakim king of Judah, Nebuchadnezzar king of Babylon came to Jerusalem and besieged it." He is no doubt quoting the scribe-chronicler, the equivalent of our TV newscaster, as he gives the bare who, what, when, and where of the event. From the human perspective all we can see is the initiative of a man. Man is in the center of the stage and God is nowhere in the circumference because, as far as the news media is concerned, God is not a relevant factor in what happens. The man behind the microphone sees only the results. What he does not see are the intangible yet real determinative principles, which, because they are based on God's unchanging absolutes, are the direct cause of the results he is reporting.

In the second verse Daniel soars to give us the divine perspective—"And the Lord delivered Jehoiakim . . . into [Nebuchadnezzar's] hand." While the news reporter sees only the Nebuchadnezzars, the Herods, and the Maos beating up a storm, Daniel from a higher perspective sees these same storm clouds as the chariots of the Lord's redemptive conquest. He insists that political changes are controlled and used by God for his own purposes. On this particular trip the Lord's chariot—Nebuchadnezzar's invasion army—has two goals to accomplish. Though one relates to Babylon and one to Israel, both will be taken care of at the same time.

First, God will have his truth witnessed to in Babylon; so there is a planting work for Nebuchadnezzar to do. The motivation of God in this world's affairs is redemptive; he desires all to be saved and come to a knowledge of the truth. For this mission he needs and has chosen to use people to be his instruments as witnesses and intercessors. Babylon is on God's heart just as Nineveh was when he sent Jonah to preach there. But where is he to get a man? In a spirit of unrelenting isolationism, the people of Israel have detached themselves from any responsibility toward the nations surrounding them.

So then God's goal for Israel is twofold: to punish her flagrant sins and also to correct this isolationism. It is at this point in history that God deliberately turns over the sovereignty of the nations to heathen kings—under his supreme control, of course—for a predetermined duration and for a designed end.

The tragedy in Judah and the evacuation of the shekinah glory from the temple in Jerusalem, a city "set in the midst of the nations," is not an indication that God is throwing in the sponge and abdicating his control—far from it! It is just that God is changing his work pattern. The light that was at the center is now to be scattered out into the darkness, and God has his eye on Daniel, Hananiah, Mishael, and Azariah to be the spearhead for his new missionary approach. His selected team of faithful, fearless witnesses will be taken to their mission field at Nebuchadnezzar's expense, by his army. And at the same time the decreed punishment will fall on Israel. God here uses the same instrument to do the punishing and the planting.

We revert to our earlier question. How do you pray when the future suddenly becomes a dead-end street? Daniel has taught us that above the dead-end streets of human perspective is the divine perspective that unfolds limitless opportunities within the will of God. God fulfills himself in many ways. Jonah's witness might be given on the street corners of Nineveh, but Daniel's band had to give theirs in the fire and in the lions' den. In both places the results were dramatic and effective. Nowhere is the greatness of God seen to such advantage as it is in his ability to use as his chariot of conquest the circumstances that pose the greatest threat to his cause.

31

Smiths, Spoilers, and Soldiers

No Victory for Weaponless Soldiers

"Under the spreading chestnut tree
The village smithy stands"—empty.

The account in 1 Samuel 13:17-22 calls our attention to Israel's empty smithies: "Not a blacksmith could be found in the whole land of Israel," verse 19 tells us. The story, in fact, revolves around the relationship between three groups of people—smiths, spoilers, and soldiers.

The smiths: In peacetime the blacksmiths hammered out plowshares, pitchforks, and mattocks. In wartime the role of the blacksmith changed. The "muscles of his brawny arm" were then needed for the creation of swords and spears.

The spoilers: The purpose of spoilers, or raiding parties, in wartime was to fight and forage. Jonathan's attack on the enemy garrison stung them and provoked them to seek revenge. Not only so, but the spoilers needed to resupply their garrison, which was inside Israel's borders.

In this passage we see the spoilers raiding settlements deep in Israel's territory with hardly a hint of opposition. Why? Because Israel was weaponless. The spoilers had already disposed of the village blacksmiths in the way warring men are supposed to dispose of those who pose a threat to their victory plans—"otherwise the Hebrews will make swords or spears" (v. 19).

The soldiers: Plenty of mighty men in Israel were well trained in warfare. But the line of battle was no place for weaponless soldiers. So when the Philistines invaded, they scattered like rats scuttling to leave a sinking ship.

Soldiers denied the means for making war are already defeated. Victories are not won with bare hands.

The Bible reverts consistently to battle language in both the Old and the New Testaments. The Lord is spoken of as a man of war who will fight, and fight he does. Moses records certain situations from "the book of the wars of the Lord." Joshua is confronted by the commander of the army of the Lord with his sword drawn.

A materialistic generation is not at home with war concepts. But if this is the language of God, it is high time we started to learn his language and to understand what he means.

A nation carries on warfare on two fronts: the front line, where there is direct contact with the enemy, and the home front, where weapons are forged and munitions prepared. The same is true in Christian warfare. Like the Philistine spoiler, the devil concentrates one part of his attention at the battlefront; the other part he reserves for the smiths, the prayer warriors, on the home front. It is true, in fact, that "Satan trembles when he sees the weakest saint on his knees"—for he knows that there weapons are forged for his defeat.

If Satan can lull spiritual weapons makers into crying, "Peace, peace, when there is no peace," and divert them to peacetime pursuits, he knows the front-line attack will disintegrate. Immobilized smiths mean demoralized soldiers.

The person on the home front has no right to expect different terms of life from that of the missionary. Spiritual wars are lost when two standards are set up—peacetime standards at home and war conditions at the front. We like to think that all who are lucky enough to escape God's draft can with clear consciences live to themselves in freedom from war's claims. Rather the call is for the smiths at the home base to embrace God's priority and get busy forging weapons for soldiers battling at the front.

Born for Battle
31 Studies on Spiritual Warfare

R. Arthur Mathews

With a foreword by Alan Redpath

The author calls Christians into spiritual battle—a challenge to attack! The chapters have been arranged as a month's daily readings to enable the reader the more easily to digest these powerful messages.

'The whole tone of these chapters is one which is sadly missing today . . . My prayer is that this book may not only have a wide circulation, but that it may become prescribed reading for all young believers, especially those contemplating ministry.'

—*Alan Redpath*

ISBN 0-903843-57-9

OM PUBLISHING
Carlisle, U.K.

Foundations of the Faith

Stuart Briscoe

Foundations of the Faith is an exciting new series from a popular and widely-travelled pastor aimed at faithful, practical and incisive exposition of key Christian teaching. Versatile, these studies can be used for personal devotions and group study.

Titles in the series:

The Fruit of the Spirit
Cultivating Christian Character
ISBN 1-85078-144-3

The Ten Commandments
Playing by the Rules
ISBN 1-85078-145-1

The Apostles' Creed
Beliefs that Matter
ISBN 1-85078-171-0

OM PUBLISHING
Carlisle, U.K.

Back to Basics
The Anatomy of a Slogan

David Porter

With a foreword by David Alton MP

Despite the collapse of the 'Back to Basics' campaign, many wish that the slogan could have meant more than the aimless charade that it became. John Major did touch a deep chord in the nation.

'In this highly readable book, David Porter spells out the real meaning of "Back to Basics". Challenging to politicians of all faiths, it is essential reading for Christians committed to citizenship of both Kingdom and world.'

—*Martyn Eden, **Evangelical Alliance***

'What has been missing so far in the "Back to Basics" debate, and what David Porter provides in this book, is the balanced approach of Christian ethics.'

—*David Alton MP*

ISBN 1-85078-155-9

OM PUBLISHING
Carlisle, U.K.

Restoring the Image

Roger Hurding

Amidst the plethora of books on counselling, here is a clear treatment of the subject for the non-specialist, covering every aspect of life, including adolescence, singleness, early years of marriage, as well as divorce and bereavement.

'Unlike many books on counselling [this] is free from the psychiatric and theological jargon guaranteed to send the reader into reverse gear . . . This is readable.'

—*Ann Townsend*, **Life of Faith**

'Well presented, psychologically authentic and scriptural.'

—*Churchman*

ISBN 1-85078-138-9

OM PUBLISHING
Carlisle, U.K.

Passion and Purity
How to Bring Your Love Life under Christ's Control

Elisabeth Elliot

'Warmly personal . . . *Passion and Purity*
couldn't be more timely, more on target.'
—*Ruth Bell Graham*

'This book is definitely for men too'
—*Billy Graham*

Through letters, diary entries and recollections of
her courtship and marriage to Jim Elliot, his
widow candidly shares the temptations,
difficulties, victories and sacrifices of two young
people whose commitment to Christ took priority
over their love for each other.

Revealing personal glimpses, combined with
relevant biblical teaching, provide realistic
guidance in today's climate of confused and
compromising moral standards. Areas covered
include dating, singleness or marriage, virginity
and chastity, men and women's roles, and
putting God first in relationships

ISBN 1-85078-147-8

OM PUBLISHING
Carlisle, U.K.

OM PUBLISHING

OM Publishing specializes in popular paperbacks in three vital areas of the church's work:

EVANGELISM
DISCIPLESHIP
MISSION

In addition, OM Publishing spearheaded the 'Pray for the World' campaign, led by the titles *Operation World* and *You Can Change the World*.

For a free catalogue, write now to:

OM Publishing, PO Box 300, Carlisle, Cumbria CA3 0QS, UK.

OM PUBLISHING
Carlisle, U.K.

020   3788   0447

AWARE

editor, John Allan

In-depth articles
Now 48 pages
New design
Bi-monthly

'It's readable, informative, never predictable and constantly encouraging the reader to think more clearly about Christian commitment.'

—*Doug Barnett*

'A thoughtful, intelligent magazine that attempts to make sense of an increasingly senseless society. An important resource for the world-aware Christian.'

—*Stewart Henderson*

ISSN 0017-8217

For a free sample, write now to Ruth Slater at:

Paternoster Periodicals, PO Box 300, Carlisle, Cumbria CA3 0QS, UK

PATERNOSTER PERIODICALS
Carlisle, U.K.